D'ARC UNDERGROUND

&

OTHER PLAYS
BY JACK RANDOM

RANDOM PLAYS, VOLUME I

CROW DOG PRESS
TURLOCK CA USA

D'ARC UNDERGROUND

& OTHER PLAYS BY JACK RANDOM

RANDOM PLAYS, VOLUME I

Published by
Crow Dog Press
1241 Windsor Court
Turlock CA 95380

Copyright 2016 Ray Miller

All rights reserved. No part of this book may be reproduced in any form or by any means, electronic or mechanical, including photocopying, recording, or by any information storage and retrieval system, without permission in writing from the publisher.

Cover art by das schlingel and Ray Miller.

ISBN-13: 978-0997788327
ISBN-10: 0997788321

D'ARC UNDERGROUND

&

OTHER PLAYS

BY

JACK RANDOM

PLAYWRIGHT'S NOTE

I have always wanted to be a writer. From the age I became capable of thinking of these matters, when other kids were deciding to be soldiers, police officers, doctors and lawyers, I knew I would always write. During my senior year in high school, I was cast in productions of *Pinocchio*, *The Fantasticks* and *A Lion in Winter*. I fell in love with the theater and began writing plays.

The first twenty years of my writing experience centered on playwrighting. I wrote, produced, directed and acted in my first full-length play in 1974. *The Continuing Story of Fosdick and Muldoon* was staged in my father's arena and was well reviewed and received.

I relocated to New York City in 1975 with the idea of capitalizing on the nation's bicentennial with an ambitious historical trilogy: *Reason's Reckoning: The Age of Tom Paine*. That project received some interesting feedback from the New York and New Jersey Shakespeare Festivals but it never found its way to the stage. I later rewrote *Reason's Reckoning* into a two-person play.

In general, my plays tend to lack action. They are more-or-less word plays and despite my intermittent effort they could not inspire theaters to engage them. I nevertheless continued to write for the stage until I moved from California to Nashville, Tennessee, in the early nineties. While there I wrote the last of my plays, including *Nashville Round* and *D'Arc Underground: A Jazz Play in 16 Choruses*. The latter was produced as a radio production in concert with my good friend and co-conspirator James Wisniewski, AKA Wiz. We performed excerpts of that work in various poetry venues from Nashville to San Francisco.

I transitioned from plays to fiction toward the end of my five-year stay in Nashville. When my short story "Burning Churches" was published in AIM Magazine I realized that there was a greater market for my fiction. I later published my first novel *Ghost Dance Insurrection* and decided to leave playwrighting behind. While I still loved the theater it seemed clear the theater did not return my affection.

The plays in this collection are what they are. I make no apologies and hope that they will strike the interest of some enterprising artistic director. Should any theater wish to stage any of these works, you will find they are available at a fair price: Free.

Jack Random
July 4, 2016

TABLE OF CONTENTS

D'Arc Underground: A Jazz Play in Sixteen Choruses	9
Fosdick & Muldoon (The Continuing Story)	49
Nighthawks Café (The Boulevard of Broken Dreams)	107
Geronimo's Revenge	153
Queen of the Lonely Hearts	209

D'ARC UNDERGROUND

A JAZZ PLAY IN 16 CHORUSES

SETTING

A dark, windowless room with three mikes for three actors and a fourth for the narrator/musician/technician who controls all sound and light at a tech center supplied with instruments and various sound machines. There are three large video monitors behind and above them.

CHARACTERS

A1: Voice of an underground radio station, broadcasting daily to the dregs of an underground world. Dressed and groomed as one would expect of a world without luxury.
A2: His haggard loyal partner.
D'ARC: Leather goddess and guest of the Underground. She is stunning in a grunge punk rock way.
NARRATOR: A technician.

D'Arc Underground was originally recorded as a radio play in an old one-room schoolhouse outside of Nashville, Tennessee, with the following cast:

> Narrator & Technician: Jim Wisniewski (aka wZ)
> A1: Joe Speer
> A2: Ray Miller
> D'Arc: Rhonda Coullet

GLOSSARY

[Note: Generations removed from the dominant society, the language of the Underground has evolved.]

A R Z, ARZ: Possessive "ours" – pronounced "Aye Are Zee" or "arz".

Balls: Generally refers to eyeballs; lower balls is self-explanatory.

Beeps: Byproducts of industrial waste – a subset of the Dregs, includes Rez, Scum and Droogies.

Brain: Know.

Brainsage: Know and understand.

Dregs: Outcasts on the surface and in the Underground, includes Scumbags, Beeps and Rez.

Gogo: General affirmation (go-go).

Lobes: Reference to ears or brain.

Nogo: General negation (no-go).

Rez: Residue of filth and grime; subset of the outcasts in the Underground.

Righteous: The ruling elite living in guarded towers on the surface of the planet.

Sage: Understand.

Scumbags, Scum, Bags: A subset of outcasts in the Underground, including A1 and A2.

U R Z: Possessive "yours" (pronounced: You Are Zee).

ACT ONE

NARRATOR: The time is the past that is the future. A mere fraction of the human race has escaped the earth's realm in search of more habitable climes. Fully a quarter of the remaining populace is underground. A legacy of crime and punishment, the crimes three generations removed and long forgotten, an endless maze of subterranean rock tunnels and living quarters, no bars, no guards, no wardens or supervisors, they define their own existence. The only reminder of their cultural birth the one-way video cameras mounted to the ceilings of the original prison structure on the upper tiers. The walls of former guard stations are lined with monitors.

CHORUS I
(Gong and jazz rises and falls to under)

[A1 and A2 appear on separate giant television screens]

A1: We are the scum that crawls out the cracks of America's nightmare.
A2: We are the byproducts of industrial waste.
A1: We are the residue of filth and grime.
A2: We are the dregs of technologic crime.
A1: What shall we do with our dirty little children?
A2: Drop em down a hole.
A1: No deposit, no return.
A2: Let's see how far they fall.
A1: No deposit, no return.
A2: What shall we do with the Beeps and the Rez?
A1: Let's drop em down a hole!
A2: No deposit, no return.

RANDOM PLAYS

A1: What shall we do with the Scum and the Dregs?
A2: Let's see how far they fall!
A1: No deposit, no return.
A2: What shall we do with the Jews and the Spades?
A1: With the Niggers and the Spicks?
A2: With the Chinks and the Rags?
A1: With the Skins and the Raves?
A2: Let's drop em down a hole!
A1: No deposit, no return.
A2: Let's see how far they fall!
A1: No deposit, no return.
A2: Curses on your Halls of Just!
A1: Curses on your Robes!
A2: Curses on your Blue Bellies!
A1: Curses on your Lobes!
A2: The downer we fall, the upper we rise!
A1: What say the Beeps?
A2: They join you, brother Scum.
A1: What say the Rez?
A2: Brother, we are one.
A1: What say me brothers all?
A2: Yo! He man! Praise the fall!
A1: Let it be so.

CHORUS II
(Gong and Jazz)

A2: The Rez are plotting, brother. The Beeps are waffle.

A1: Let them plot. Let them waffle. Who holds the offering?

A2: Chill, A1, the offering be A R Z.

A1: Seek and see, A2, he that holds the strange true brew, the upper the up, the downer the down, will rule.

A2: For now, A1, but if the tunnel buzz be tried and true, the Beeps will follow the lead and bumpity bump the Bags will fall. The Rez they say offer up a new strange brew. The rumble will stumble flat the old and gray the ocean blue.

A1: The rise is in the fall. Scumbag rule is unity. The Rez will space and chuck us all in the Doggie Diner dungheep. The Beeps will not follow.

A2: The Beeps follow their noses.

A1: Sniff it out, brother. Sniff it, snort it, sneeze it out and bring it back down home.

A2: Can and will, A1 true blue. Chill!

A1: Chill!

[Jazz starts low and builds]

A1: He worries too much I sage. His brain be scorch and burn. I am the A1 wonder sauce. I am the big bacon cheese wiz. Rez bleed and drop like flies. Banana boys with their bimbo bebops top me not I sage. The bonzo rebel glories in bogus bonfires. The downer the fall, the greater the rise. Seek dissent, embrace demise! Can't touch me now, bugle boys. I breathe the putrid stench of dirt, disease and drudge. I sniff the dung of dogs. I lick the sludge of slimy sloth. I drink the puss of sores. Touch me not, I sage. Still, better safe that sorrow full. So say the saints of syphilis: I gots it to keeps from getting it. I plot, I plan, I spy, I scan, my eyes are always everywhere. No move is make without my knowing. No scheme is hatch without my showing. The Rez be flighty fluttery things. Beeps be sheeps. Scumbags rule!

CHORUS III
(Gong and Jazz)

A1: What's with this shit? The buzz be diddle dee and diddle dumb. The skuzz be jack!

A2: The curse be upon us. It spreads like nuclear disease. All the offerings go flat. The Rez are rumble and roar. The Beeps are bust. The bitch is a witch they say.

RANDOM PLAYS

A1: What bitch is this?

A2: A leathered hag. She drops in slick as slime and grooves us jazz in B flat minor: "Take me to the man," she bops. "The man don't take no bitches in," says I. "The bitches come to him when fingers snap." The bitch don't take no shit but throws it back in double time. Jazz be ripe in rhyme. The bitch be fine as ruby red wine.

A1: Mark it, post and let it fly: What's the bitch got to do with the Nogo high?

A2: Nada, zero, zilch, I sage, but as she rants and raves the spirits fly and all goes flat before her eye. The bitch be acid queen and masters everything it seems she touches. Who brains what curse her spirits bring?

A1: Bring her before me and let her sing or crumble, rust and die. Nogo to the one who snuffs the righteous high!

A2: I go but listen well: All that breaks down here the vidcam will tell and sure as mud on rainy daze, the buzz goes up and trickles down again. Mark it, A1, and scan: If anyone sets the bitch down, you can. I bend and shuffle triple time but sage, A1: D'Arc be no common slut.

[Jazz building]

A1: This bitch fires me and pumps my blood red hot. Thunderbolt and lightning, burn baby burn! She sparks the ancient ashes to raging flame. Scorch the parchment black baby black! Can the bitch be witch? Can she lift the buzz from sacred root? Uncommon slut indeed but if she turns my water wine then plot be fine and D'Arc be just what Scumbags need.

[Enter A2 with D'ARC]

A2: The bitch be U R Z.

D'ARC: D'Arc be no manchild's pet. Shift your squinty

balls and sage it well. Twist, climb, squirm and scramble up a ring, rise your puny conscious brain, the spirit's call you. Shall you waste wonder lost and stone the meaning? Cool breeze baby blue. The why-because is you for me and me for you, A1.

A1: The why-because is no go like the high that was before. Can you witch the water wine, bitch? Can you straight the crook, you haggard leather fiend? Can you hoist the fingered high?

D'ARC: Your high is baby piddle. Your brain is buzzed dry and shrivel. Petting lap dogs and sucking sugar sticks. You cod mouthed dimble wit! There are no bitches here save she that licks her underside and cleans your oiled paws.

A1: Eye it nose and ear, these paws bare claws for bitches who oppose! But slate it blank and let it fly. My brain is daze. The why-because it has no fuel! The cool breeze blows away. Jazz be the wind! The offering goes dry.

D'ARC: You sniffling, sniveling scumbag.

[D'ARC produces the sacred seed from a leather pouch around her waist]

D'ARC: Feast your balls. Nose it, mouth and stomach it: The seeds of true blue jazz in B flat minor. Jazz be U R Z if the cause be just and righteous be the cause.

A1: Who be the judge of what be just and true?

D'ARC: That be me for I am here to show it you and serve, a warrior for the cause of one, a soldier for the one true blue.

A1: I take and wait the witching hour.

D'ARC: Do and call me when you're through.

[A1 takes the sacred seed and reclines]

CHORUS IV

RANDOM PLAYS

(Gong and Jazz)

[A1 on a giant television screen]

A1: Glory and praise for she that raise the offering! The lights dance and spirits space the night. The high returns to us and crowns our queen!

A2: [chant] Morphine heroin cocaine eucidol diloidid pantipone diosane hashish opium Demerol dolophine morphine...

A1: We are the scum that crawls out of the cracks of America's nightmare! They fear us because we're alive despite them! They shake and quiver because our souls survive to fight them! We are their betters before the eyes of their own gods. We are the stronger because of them. The scum shall inherit the earth, the underbelly of soul and sickliness. We are the nightmare they can't escape! They shelter us in the belly of the beast and think of us no more. Rattle and quake! Thunder and roar! Let them feel your righteous wrath beneath their shivering feet! Tremble and die! Your tears cannot save you now! Yield and make your peace! Time and the hour is upon you! Scumbags rule!

D'ARC: Praise and glory be yours, A1. The story unfolds as written.

[A1 continues chant under as A2 appears on the screen]

A2: We are the byproducts of industrial wastelands! We be the enemies of the Righteous Ones! Not because we threaten the safety of their streets! We be the enemy because we defy their way of life! We do not fit the molds of their society. We create our own rules and mark our own passage! We reject your offering of crumbs and offer up our own!

A1: You've done it their way and didn't dig it! You've had what they gave you and couldn't take it! You've been there and left, seen it and closed your eyes, begged for it, got it and threw in the dungheep because it wasn't quite what it was supposed to be! You joined and dropped out. You told them you cared and knew you didn't. You swore you believed, you believed, you believed until you found out they spoke a different language! Didn't you? You stood in their unemployment lines, lived in their slums, tasted their cockroaches, slept with their rats, and you watched your brothers get drafted and shafted, and you watched your sisters get fouled and fooled, and you've had your fill of it! So you looked around, searching, hoping, finally found the Underground. Jump down, brothers, embrace the fall! Jump down sisters, yield to the call! Brain be the cause, sage be the light, Scumbags rule!

D'ARC: Shill be the thrill, you brainless fools, the high is nigh, the buzz be in your head.

A1: Jump down, sister, burn baby burn!

[D'ARC appears on the screen surrounded by a glow]

D'ARC: The junkie has no art. The spirit has no heart. The unfed soul is bled dry.

A2: Sing it, sister, the high is nigh!

D'ARC: Freedom is to poetry what night is to the blind.

A1: Weigh it, sister, bleed it dry!

D'ARC: The creative force be one!

A2: Jazz be the word! Bring it back down home!

D'ARC: The drive will hold you down and bind you to the holy ground and call you childish knaves and bid you seek the flaws of cause surround you like a cloud.

A1: Leathered truth, black baby black!

D'ARC: Gravity is the force of higher mind.

A2: Scat baby scat!

D'ARC: Travel to the ends of understanding.

A1: Dark baby dark!

D'ARC: Crash and burn, oh worried ones, turn back

promises, sacrifice yourself to save your soul.
    A2: Down baby down!
    D'ARC: I am here to raise you to the light!
    A1-2: Chill!

CHORUS V
(Gong and Jazz)

    A1: [pacing, in chamber] Who are you that stokes my underground and stands my staff alert? No bitch before so feeds the fuel that tempts my fire rages. Brain be ponder what dark desire sages. Be the bitch witch, wiz or spirit downer still?

    D'ARC: [entering] Hear and sage or brain be purple haze and maze to wander lost. I am no bitch. I am no wiz, no witch, no spirit plaything for A1 wonder kind to finger slime and slam. Lift your sorry balls from lower view and cruise the upper light. I am she with ear and core, brain and heart to dig the voices heaven sent. The power that be mine be channeled forth from ancient time to stamp your simple minds with burn and wonder glory.

    A1: Jazz be fine oh dark and leathered one but plot and story trail like moon to sunlight. What be these voices? Who be the heaven sender?

    D'ARC: Heaven be one. The upper the up and down the voices come. Their names be sacred roll and thunder clap. Beat of three and perfect harmony. Their words be bottom line: Seek the A1 wonder kind for he alone is chosen.

    A1: Brain be whys? Why do spirits finger me the A1 Scumbag king? Praise be glory rabble raise yet jam no licks my way? If I be he that leads and follows none, why send a leathered hag to beat my drum? Wise be the whys that tell me no go – not to follow blind and diddle dumb but question, pause and brain this spirit jive. Sage the jazz that sings the hidden cause.

JACK RANDOM

D'ARC: Question, brother, brain and be not dumb or blind. The voices sing to you for me in jazz be ever always kind. Lobe and heart the beat of dungeon deep and tried true tunnel black and ocean blue. The upper the up, the higher the high, and jazz to he that flies.

A1: This trumpet sounds a sour chord. The upper the up, the downer the down, this be creed and holy ground. The downer the down, the upper the up, remove us from the Righteous Ones who bleed us dry and pick our flesh from bone. Scumbags rule in darkness! All sage begins with this.

D'ARC: Sage again, A1. Brain and double. The time be right, the moment knock and enter. Rise be the tide and moon be pull! The Righteous Ones be shake and hide behind their babble tower walls of barren rock and bury them in air. Quake and quiver be their affliction! The people rise and rumble roam the streets! The time be ripe, the moment knock and enter!

A1: Brain be burn and balls be wonder filled. Patch the quilt and bring it down! Scan the plan and serve it whole.

D'ARC: Rise! The way be up! The air be U R Z to nose and palm! The people rally to your drum and strike them down the granite walls, the tower babble falls!

A1: Jazz be far and distant sound, the surface will not rally to the Underground.

D'ARC: They rally now behind your tunnel view. They talk the talk, they walk the walk and drive the jive down home. Jazz be U R Z and praise! The cam be the scam, the video craze and lays it at your feet.

A1: What scam be this that raise my praise with my knowing? The cam be underground and down and out she goes to Beeps and Rez and Scumbag brothers; no go to the surface high.

D'ARC: They watch you, brother. They steal your view. The Righteous Ones turn you on to pacify and profit but bumpity bump the beat is strong, they fear they cannot turn you off again. Surface Dregs be born and grow in lore and shakes them at the tower door: A1! they bark. Scum be rise and rule once more!

A1: Jazz be strange and twisted too. Cool be the cam that scam the jam and stick it in their nose! The numbers grow above that look to those below. Jazz be vengeance tried and true.

D'ARC: No go, nada, zero, zed. Jazz be justice vengeance led. Might be right and freedom's call. As Scumbags rise, the Righteous Ones be fall.

A1: The word be Gogo! The seed be strong. Jazz be justice; freedom be the song.

D'ARC: Cool breeze ocean blue, jam the scam and rise. Scumbags rule!

A1: Pause and ponder, brain be turn to here and now. The way be block and stone be endless barrier. The passage up is Nogo.

D'ARC: Voices tell the how and mark the when. The when be now. The how be in the moss that upper grows upon the northeast wall.

A1: Rhyme the riddle, Dark One, the time be gone for wonder.

D'ARC: Find the moss that upper grows. There plant your tunnel techies and drive. The way be circle up and rise.

[D'ARC bows and exits]

A1: The way be clear if voices tell no lies. The tunnel rats be search and seek. The plot be plan and hatch and spread the word and jazz be wise. If not, the way be wary and Dark One be demise.

CHORUS VI
(Gong and Jazz)

A2: The upper moss be found, the tunnel techies drive.

JACK RANDOM

The bitch be witch and brain be hers that no one else can sage.

A1: She is no bitch. She is the dark and leathered hag of Scumbag dreams. If witch she be, what care am I? She leads me to the upper high.

A2: She be the big bopper cheese wiz. Can't touch her now. Holy ground be she and wonder goddess of the night. Moon be too small for her light. She be the stars that Scumbags, Rez and Dregs but dream of and brain by vision on high! The Beeps are hers and Rez be turning. When the bitch can point the upper way and sage the true blue offering, what need be Dregs for you and I?

A1: I am fingered A1 wonder kind and king! The voices be her sage and they be pledge to me.

A2: For now, A1, for now, but when she palms the offering and techies break to open sky, who brains what songs her voices sing? Jazz be praise and glory tonight but what be lock and key to sing your fall by daylight?

A1: Shake and tremble not, A2, we hold the offering. It grows and flourish in hallowed ground. The offering be A R Z!

A2: It grows for all but spirits fly at witch's call.

A1: I sage the D'Arc One's magic, stomach and heart, true to the blue, A2. She will not turn but care and comfort be the wind. Seek it out, A2. Let's find the spark of voices D'Arc.

A2: Sage A1 and tremble not. The trickle down is doom. The word that marks my brain in blood red daggers goes up and out and scatters. The residue be soon. Ready and steady, A1, heart sage and brain the maze. This D'Arc One palms your balls! Clear your vise and ready. The cause be action and action be the cause.

A1: Scope it, brother, let it fly! The upper the up, the higher the high! Chill!

A2: Chill!

RANDOM PLAYS

[Exit A2 ... Jazz]

A1: Bitch be witch not I sage. Cause be push and serve to let them heart and brain she be. So long as she be cause and serve to me, can she be whore to Righteous kind? Not I sage but brain be wise and trust not the fire set in root and core. She is no whore to my desire! She turns my hot to cold and blows it hot once more. Burn baby burn! The voices be the lock and key. If they be real, they will not stumble, trip and fall on D'Arc desire. If they be false, soon they sing a D'Arc demise. Plot be the plan, study and devise, the test that best will serve. If she be true and ocean blue, the upper the up, the higher the high, Dregs will rise and mark this day as mine. Scumbags rule!

CHORUS VII
(Gong and Jazz)

[Enter D'ARC as A1 reclines on bed of scattered fur and leather]

D'ARC: Rise A1 and raise the warrior cry! The tunnel buzz be wait and wonder. Stir the Dregs alive! The tunnel techies by my balls break through to morning light. The night be long, the moment be upon us.

A1: What time be this that speaks of morning light? The night be long enough for Dregs who have no sight.

D'ARC: The time be now, A1. Time enough to raise the Underground and organize the fight!

A1: The Under organize themselves by fours and fives they scatter, scramble, hide and wait for surface Dregs to follow. But these lobes till now be virgin to this news. My eyes are always everywhere. The Underground be mine. What serves you up what be not served to me.

D'ARC: The voices speak that tell no lies. The

Underground has spies who speak in double tongue and plot the fall of kings. Take care, A1. Your lobes would burn to hear the name of traitor in the midst. What more they do not tell.

A1: My lobes burn now though cause be not sage. My balls be blinded by the dark.

D'ARC: Heart, A1, and trust the flame that burns within. Voices finger you and crown you king. They bid you ready steady and rise the forces of the Underground. Jazz be true and time be ripe. Shudder and stutter not in brain be cloud and wonder. Moment be seize, hammer and fist!

A1: The Dregs be ready. Beeps, Rez and Scumbags sing harmonic praise to the D'Arc One, her hallowed voices and the sacred high.

D'ARC: The only high be rise and roar! Dregs rule and fall the Righteous Ones! Take it to the streets! Lightning strike and thunder, the surface rallies to the storm! Hide and peek like cowering dogs licking their behinds will not stir them to the cause.

A1: Caution be the wind. The Righteous Ones be warn and notice. The tower guard be ready aim and fire.

D'ARC: The number be too small. They ring around the tower rosy and steady up their wall. Can't touch us now, A1.

A1: Even numbers small can crush the cause if time and place be post and map. The cam sets all before their Righteous balls.

D'ARC: Let the time be post! It sets their Righteous hearts to shake and quiver. It fogs the Righteous brain and paralyze. The place be maze and fog. They will not dare the streets they care not who controls.

A1: If this be so, the Underground will know and roar and thunder be the cause. The surface Dregs will stir and follow Scumbags to the tower walls.

D'ARC: Cool blue ocean breeze, hot spring and rising tide, ripe and raise the rebel cry: The word be Gogo! Time be happening! Jazz be storm and thunder! With you or without you, A1 wonder kind?

A1: What tune be this that sings without my praise? Jazz be dark and scatter that stops the newborn Go that wants my blessing. I am the big bopper cheese wiz saint of no tomorrow! Treat and bury me with dust not I sage. Rot and rust! I will not yield to yellow nada zilch! Nogo!

D'ARC: The way be up! Can't stop us now. You be chosen but you must choose. Lead and we will follow. Rise and we will conquer! Wait and worry, still be the chill, and we will rise or fall without you but rise we must and will.

A1: What say the voices, D'Arc? With you or without?

D'ARC: [waits, listens] The voices be silence.

A1: Strange be the voices that push and pull and praise the thunder but wait and wonder now. Caution be the wind that moves them. Fear and trepidation.

D'ARC: You must choose. They will not choose for you.

A1: Brain be bury heart in hand, palm and fist. Deed be done. I sage the turn I take. What say the voices now?

[D'ARC waits, listens, kneels, prays]

A1: Test be place and center. See how she prays the voices do not fail her. Mind be maze. Heart be not denied. I burn to see the light and stand the D'Arc by my side. She moves me like no other. The night will come when she will burn for me as my heart burns now. Flame be the game of war and rebel. She brains my core be pause and coward. She brains my power weak and worldly. Light be the flame, spark be the fire when A1 leads the storm! But wait and balls be wonder glaze, see how she rises to the light. The voices speak, pray they be right.

D'ARC: [finally] You are with us, A1.

A1: Praise and glory, D'Arc One! Praise and glory! Voices speak true blue jazz in B flat minor!

D'ARC: Praise and glory! Time be gone for wonder.
A2: [entering] Mark it, A1: Techies break the sky!
D'ARC: Mark it, A1: Voices speak true blue!
A1: Jazz be the wind! Praise and glory!

[A1 appears at podium, his face on a giant television screen]

A1: Come, me Droogies! The high is nigh upon us! The sky is broken! The solar king awaits his chosen ones buried in the tomb of mother earth! Come, me Droogies, strike back at those who buried you for crimes you never knew and never had the pleasure of the doing! Come hand and fist, avenge your fathers and your mothers and your sisters and your brothers, dumped for spitting on their Righteous streets and banging on your drums! The time be now! The moment be arrive! Pick up your arms! Fight for your rights! Rise and rabble rouse and heed the rebel call! When Droogies be rise, the Righteous Ones be fall!

CHORUS VIII
(Gong and Jazz)

[A1 in his tunnel quarters]

A1: The day belongs to Beeps and Rez and Surface Dregs! Scumbags rule in unity and strength! The force of one be A R Z! The babble tower be circle and siege. Soon the wall be tumble and fall! Storm be rage and fury! Can't stop us now, oh Righteous Ones!
A2: Mark, A1, the word be trickle down! Wall be fall! The Guard fall back and scatter! Within the hour, the tower be A R Z!
A1: Praise and glory be, A2. Jazz be victory! Where be D'Arc in this battle?
A2: She leads the Dreggies to the Tower door. Lasers fly and raise the Dark One's hair. Her leathers scorch and

tear but she be light, wind and shadow, flies against the storm! Bitch be witch and fears no mortal harm.

    A1: If witch she be, praise and glory she stands with me. She is no Righteous whore.

    A2: Word be mum on that, A1. The trickle down be stop and start now that the underground be up. I tell you this: By these balls, they speak of her in hush and whisper and fear to mark her face to face.

    A1: Mark A2 and chill. The more they fear, the better be. She be Dreggie warrior queen but they follow me, the A1 wonder kind as king. Mark it post and let it fly: The upper the up, the higher the high.

    A2: Shake and quiver be mine, A1. D'Arc be unreal. Her voices feed beyond the stars. She be with them, one of them, beyond them, within them, they will not yield to earthly beings. Beware A1, brain the outcome and fear!

    A1: If this be true and ocean blue, caution to the wind and fly! Take it for a ride and ride it high! Nogo be the stopper now. D'Arc be Queen of Everything and trumpets sound her praise in B flat minor. Can't touch her now, A2, so let it bleed and wonder. The day be praise and glory! Jazz be sky high. Down me not with worry.

    A2: Chill be mine, A1 wonder kind. The high be true blue.

    [Enter D'ARC, flurry...]

    D'ARC: Mark it, post and fly! The tower be A R Z!

    A1: Bold be gold and pass it down to us. Tales of daring sweep the Underground and fly above. D'Arc has no fear and can't be touched by Righteous Guard or Righteous flame.

    D'ARC: The voices guide and protect the true blue warriors. We rally to the rebel cry and mark the day in victory. Jazz be post and haste. The Righteous Ones be holed and wait the word of A1 wonder kind.

A1: What say the voices on this line?

D'ARC: They yield but bid you be wise: the fist in war, the palm in triumph. Jazz be swift and mercy beat.

A2: The Righteous be root of vengeance and destroy! Pluck them up and lay them down in poison and in blood!

D'ARC: Fear be Righteous outside our call. Now they beg and steady hold behind their walls. Raise their passion and they come in rhyme and circle us. Calm and order beats our drum and stays them in their slumber.

A2: They come without our call. They will not hold and steady while we hold and steady their Righteous kind. Be done, A1, and hold and steady us for war against the tide!

A1: The way of Righteous vengeance be clear. The way of wisdom be blind. Jazz be justice and justice be poetry and rhyme. What shall we do with the Righteous kind?

A2: Let's drop 'em down a hole!

A1: No deposit, no return.

A2: Let's see how far they fall!

A1: No deposit, no return.

A2: What shall we do with the prissy little pinkies?

A1: Drop 'em down a hole!

A2: No deposit, no return.

A1: Let's see how far they fall!

A2: No deposit, no return.

A1: What shall we do with the fairy princess queens, with the bankers and the butchers, with the masses and the beans?

A2: Let's drop 'em down a hole!

A1: No deposit, no return.

A2: Let's see how far they fall!

A1: No deposit, no return.

A2: Curses on your halls of just! Curses on your robes!

A1: Curses on your blue bellies! Curses on your lobes!

All: Drop 'em down a hole, drop 'em down a hole, drop 'em down a hole...

RANDOM PLAYS

[Fade Jazz]

ACT TWO

SETTING: As before.

CHORUS IX
(Gong and Jazz)

[A1 and A2 appear on separate giant television screens]

A1: We are the scum that crawls out of the cracks in America's nightmare!
A2: We are the byproducts of industrial rage!
A1: We are the residue of hazardous waste!
A2: We are the dregs of the technologic age!
A1: Righteous Ones, take care. Surface dregs will rally everywhere and stop you in your Righteous tracks! Jazz be hold and ball the hour! Stir and crumble from your Righteous tower! Dregs will take you down! Mark it post and save! United by the dark of wonder glory, Beeps, Rez, Scum and surface dregs are one! Bold and jazz be cool blue ocean breeze. War no more! Rise and jazz be rage and thunder! Brain, sage and take it home.
A2: We demand food for hunger free of charge! We demand jobs for all who call and ones that suit their make and model, not their shoes! We demand the laser stun be drop and done or access free to all! We demand the opening of the boundaries: Free travel, an end to border stops and crossing! We demand the closing of the Righteous Guard! Let them work to feed the poor. We demand access to the stars! Let all behold the heavens and scope the upper maze. We demand a home for all and not a hole to shovel dirt in! We demand the upper the up, the higher the high, the sacred root be legalize! Our bodies and our minds be our own to

ground or rise. We demand open airways and open mainframe RAM! Access free to all! We are no fools! We sage your schools be bust and tame the brain no more. Sage and cool breeze be upon you! D'Arc and A1 Wonder Kind await you!

[D'ARC appears on screen]

D'ARC: Wise be the word! Chill and mark it well. Dregs take heed and Righteous beware. The offering be true blue square and fair. We ask no more than what be ARZ by right and true command of heaven! The voices pray be wise and sage the ancient lies that let you hold your brothers and your sisters down and bury them beneath the ground like dogs of lesser grade. The earth belongs to all who live and die by her mercy. Retrace the wrong and scope the upper way. Dregs be rise and seize the light of day! No more will they be buried! No more will they be bound and tied! No more will they be pawn to Righteous power! Dregs all and everywhere rise up and organize! Your duty and your glory calls! Scumbags rule in unity and strength!

CHORUS X
(Gong and Jazz)

[Enter A2]

A2: Chill, A1. Jazz be sorrow full. The word that lights the dark and sends it down be broke and ever always lies asleep. The trickle down be topple. The Underground be blind and cross.

A1: What jazz be this that shoulders sorrow but sings no song? No right, no wrong?

A2: The song be mourn and suffer. My brother dies from cause be no man's sage. No sight, no song, no right, no wrong but sorrow ever after. The word that lights the D'Arc for traitor choked in his throat.

A1: Brain be the word or sorrow's maze and wonder?

A2: I brain because I heart no more. She plucks it beating from my breast. My balls be ever upper rise while yours be sink below.

A1: The word be maze and sorrow wonder. My eyes be rise and scope the upper view as yours. But this touches not the D'Arc. The Righteous would take him down alone.

A2: Brain be whys? Why now and how? Brother be the line to find the Dark One out! He serves us well and long. The Underground reveals him not until darkness comes around.

A1: Wise be the whys but chill. If D'Arc make this kill, seek and find it out in cold and bloody proof! The Dregs will have no doubt. Even now she leads us in triumph and glory. They will not yield to less than all this story.

A2: Mark it, post and save. Proof be mine or dine on my remains. If D'Arc be Righteous whore, no more I say 'til I return and bend her to her Righteous knees!

A1: Chill. My heart be sorrow too but chill. Caution be the cause. If D'Arc be killer, fear she kills again. She brains too much and scopes the path before it travels.

A2: I shake and tremble not. Way be treachery and sly, I will succeed or die.

A1: Peace to the beast and guard you ever always.

[Exit A2]

A1: I fear the cause be Nogo! Fail and A1 stands alone in doubt and wonder paralyze. Succeed and face the power of the D'Arc. Bitch be witch and wronged, she will knock us down and raise the Rez instead. Bitch be witch and Righteous whore? Nada, zero, zilch I sage. She would not serve the master but the brood. Bitch be Righteous whore and nothing more? This rights my story best. Burn the bitch for witch and scumbags take the glory. Proof be in the porridge. Til then the word be mum and D'Arc be Queen of Mean and everything she fingers turns to gold.

[Jazz rise and fade under; spot on D'ARC; sound of doors and flurry]

D'ARC: Mark and steady for the storm! The Righteous Guard be raise and rouse to rumble at our door!
A1: They heed our warning not! Then close the hand that holds them in our grasp! Die be the cry to those that ear our words and take them not to heart!
D'ARC: Time be squeeze and flicker out. Screw the Righteous in our grasp and let them rot! Rally the outside Dregs to rise and stopper to the storm. Jazz be hot and take it to them! I burn to serve the cause in strike and hammer home or let me breathe no more!
A1: Righteous be the cause of flaws. Divide our forces not I sage. Power to the Tower! Dregs rule in unity and strength! Let them break our hold; outer Dregs will rally on their own.
D'ARC: They will not follow without lead! They will not rally to those who cower in the tower! Ear the voices well and heed: Steady and hold and Dregs will fold. The Righteous Guard will circle and lay siege. Rally the Surface Dregs all and everywhere or lost be the cause of just!
A1: How be this cause and reason? The voices sing to this but hold their tongues on trial for Righteous treason?
D'ARC: The voices be their own masters and choose the time and place. They be no fools. They sage the stake be high. Hold and lose or bold and raise the rebel cry and scatter be the word. The A1 wonder kind rallies to the fold! Jazz be wildfire! Scorch and thunderbolt! Sage, heed, untie my hands and let me fight!
A1: Sacred be the voices and pure. The word be heed

and Gogo! Jazz be praise and glory road! Take it to them, D'Arc, and bring it back down home.

D'ARC: Praise and glory! Scumbags rule! Raise the rebel cry and rally them to join me in this fight! I will not fail.

[Exit D'ARC]

A1: Cunning sly and shady be the Dark One now. She summons voices to her call, trembles my calm and lowers my cautious guard. If word be bounce and trickle down against her, she will outstretch my reach. Out of arms and out of harm's way. Can't touch her now, me Dreggies. She brains my cause and sage be rescue. She brains me weak and tremble. Voices be the cause! Go against and lose the tide.
Cunning sly and shady! She grabs me by the lower balls and squeeze! Squirm be the worm that feeds my rocket fuel and flies!
Still...she burns me. Flame be desire more and more. I would have the Righteous whore just once before I die. Rally be the cause and take it to the streets! Lead and organize the Dregs she leaves behind. I will play my part.

[Jazz rises and falls, continuing under. A1 on the Giant Screen with altered lighting to signify an address to the masses.]

A1: Scumbags, Beeps and Rez, Underground and Surface Dregs, chill and thrill! Fire and Ice! Jazz be charge and motion, rise and organize! D'Arc streaks to strike the Tower Guard be march and siege to circle us! Mark it, post and pass the torch to Surface Scum: The rebel cry be U R Z! Rise and follow greatness into glory! Where D'Arc leads the lasers part and scatter! Fire moves by wind of Dark desire! The Righteous Ones be awe and wonder, stumble, turn and fall! Heed the call and stake your claim to the order of the new and greater day! Dregs everywhere, steady and strong, I join you in the streets to build our defenses and dig our trenches. Plot and plan to stand before the tide and roll it back again. The voices of Darkness be with you now and ever after! Power to the Tower! The force be A R Z! Chill and readiness be praise!

[Gong. Jazz rises and falls.]

CHORUS XI
(Jazz under; A2 alone)

A2: Mark and take it to heart. Dark and weary be my bones. Ache almost to break. Am I too late? The Darkness moves with owl's grace over unsuspecting prey. Proof and positive be mine. The bitch be not witch I sage but deceit and Righteous whore be she and more. She brains our cause and weakness and works her magic by sly and cunning shift of hand and sight. By dark passage we sage this platform be all the cam can scan. Nada, zero, zilch! The walls have balls and ears and tongues to tell our all and every motion. The Underground be open to the Tower Techies. Our plot and plan be pipe to Righteous hand. To save themselves they turn our smoke to flame. Burn baby burn! The hand that feeds you now fingers you to blame. Jazz be vengeance hot and bittersweet! Vengeance be mine, hand, palm and fist!
But am I too late? Jazz be patience tempered by fear. By second sight, I sense the Darkness near.

[Enter D'ARC]

D'ARC: Stun be the gun and wary! [pause to scope the scene] Where be A1 Wonder Kind? Time be roll and thunder!
A2: I sage he plays the Warrior King of Light and

Darkness and readies Surface Dregs to fight the coming wave. What news beyond our reach?

D'ARC: Their numbers play the maze and baffle. We raise the stopper here. They fold and scatter. To the left and right they streak toward the prize. Again we rise and blaze to meet them hand and foot. Again they scatter. They will not fight us on the open ground. We back and rally to make a final stand.

A2: Where be the Surface Dregs to rise and stop the tide?

D'ARC: They rally to my cry and not divide. They slow the shifting wave but cannot stopper.

A2: Where be the voices in this dark and dizzy battle?

D'ARC: They leave us to our own device and wait our choices.

A2: Caution be the wind that blows your voices now. Hold and steady, ready for the fall.

D'ARC: The voices test our hearts. Freedom be no bargain but a prize. Faith and will combined will turn this tide. Divide and we will shatter. The stuff of puff and powder will fall. Stuff be strong and greatness rise to grab the cherished prize.

A2: And place the Darkness above the tide.

D'ARC: [pause] I brain your balls be sly and hide a cunning mind. I sage your mind be turn and dagger. I know the seed and take your sorrow home. Pause be the cause: I am not guilty of this deed!

A2: Name my suffering and give me cause to pause.

D'ARC: I know his color, not his name. Your brother's killer be Righteous Underground and takes no offering.

A2: You be wise or cunning most or both. Brain be daze and dazzle. How now come you by this knowing?

D'ARC: My eyes are open always. More I cannot say. But hold and stay the course. All will out and open when jazz be contemplate and settle this account.

A2: I hold and still the night. Cause be mine as yours. I will not would not rush to judgment.

D'ARC: Cool blue and ocean breeze. Then fly and post the A1 wonder kind: Bid him come to plan the stand. I stay behind and ready for his word.

A2: Chill. He will appear before the hour tire.

D'ARC: Praise be glory.

[Exit A2]

CHORUS XII

(Gong and Jazz rises and falls, sound of wind under)

D'ARC: Dark be the moon and blood cloud sky. He brains me traitor false by true account. I am no witch but warrior for the cause true blue. Silent voices cross my brow, tie and bind me to the stake, hammer and nail. Burn baby burn! The Righteous Ones thrive by word be Nogo and turn my balls upper inward.

[Kneels and prays]

Humble be the cause and flaws that blind me to the light and lay me at your gate. I am your warrior! Bold and pure be the heart of D'Arc! Loyal, true and giving be my soul. Service me again with second sight and voices be my guide. The hour is need. Winds of rage whip the night and cover them with dust! Plague be hard and curse the Righteous Guard with weak resolve! Ill-tempered will and sickness strike them down and hold to give us time. All is not lost…when freedom be the cost…and hands above be joined to hearts below.

[Sound of doors opening, closing, flurry; enter A1]

A1: Rise and greet your Warrior King! Our numbers grow and rally to the rebel cry! Our readiness be near. Even now the winds swirl and turn the Righteous Guard inside itself and stop them in their tracks. Time be ARZ! Cool blue and ocean breeze.

D'ARC: Glory, praise and wonder! The heavens be with us once more.

A1: The heavens be with and against it seems. Horns blow with shifting wind and voices sing the harmony. Jazz be flighty, fickle, frail. Come and go. Yes and Nogo. Inconstant be the stars that guide us.

D'ARC: Waver not in faith. The voices fail us not, I sage, but move us to the edge of greatness! Warrior be not brave, I sage, if fate be in his palm and fist. Jazz be just. Freedom be the cause! No less the price we pay.

A1: Word be righteous and righteous be the word that serves the cause of just. Freedom be the dream that thrives inside the righteous high! The offering be ARZ! Offer up and serve.

[D'ARC produces the sacred seed]

D'ARC: Praise glory! The high is in your head but down the sacred seed to ready you for battle!

A1: Praise be the light of Dark! The upper the up, the higher the high, join me in this flight! Righteous be the one that takes no offering.

D'ARC: I join and follow ocean into sky. Praise be A1 wonder kind and King!

[They take the sacred offering. Jazz flurry rise and fade.]

CHORUS XIII
(Gong and Jazz under)

A1: Join me in this flame that will not wait the night! Open and divide to seal our unity. Jazz be lickety split and bumpity bump and grind! Burn me to the higher high and ready me for war as no man can! The A1 wonder kind would have his Queen!

D'ARC: D'Arc be Warrior would be no man's Queen! Push no more, A1. I will not yield and open to your drive!

A1: Jazz be tease and squeeze the lower balls to bust! Leather be the cause of flaws that torch and burn my yearn to dive inside! Torture me with praise and stay me from desire?

D'ARC: Will not would not could not blame not, shame and wonder! Pause be the cause that blinds you from your purpose. Raise your lower balls to high once more and ready you for war! There be no other cause.

A1: Mark it from this time: The A1 wonder kind stands alone in glory and in war! Voices of the Dark be damned! The Dregs will rally to my call and Righteous Ones with D'Arc will fall!

D'ARC: Strength be unity! Pause to brain the cause.

A1: Cause of flaws be damned! Unity be break and scatter with the dust! You are fingered, Dark One! Witch and Righteous whore! Make haste and fly! The clouds be lowered. Thunderbolt and lightning streak the sky! Heaven's voices sing to A1 wonder kind and cry: The Dark One must die!

D'ARC: Cause be crash and burn! I am no man's whore! I flee no man's wrath and fear no man's scorn! I seek the cause of just and will be justified. But now I fight and bring my right to bear! Shake and tremble, A1! Shame be the why-because that fingers me with blame!

A1: Crash and burn, Dark and Righteous One! The high is nigh. Scuz be the buzz! The Righteous Ones abandon you and feed your seed with nada, zero, zilch! The offering goes flat once more! The Dregs will not follow. Brain, sage and fly! Jazz be save yourself.

D'ARC: The high be ever always in your mind. I go but do not fly! The battle cry is call and beckons me. Day be done and battle won, I stand to meet the charge.

[Doors open and close as D'ARC exits; spot fades.]

A1: She mouths the cause but takes it not to heart. She brains the wiser course and flies. We will not lay our balls on Darkness ever more. I stomach it to pain and bitter pill. Bleed and suffer tries my warrior soul. Worship be the heart of D'Arc in mine. Even now she fuels my fire! Burn baby burn! I rise and fight the Righteous tide 'til breath be in and out no more! Justice be the cause! Dreggies in unity, hand and fist! Scumbags rule!

[Gong and scat jazz rise and fade]

CHORUS XIV
(Jazz rises and falls; continues under)

A1: Scum of the earth! Rise and conquer! Dreggies under and over unite and stake your claim! Heart and fist be ARZ! The outer Righteous Guard with laser cannon beast of steel stutter and stumble at our door! They have no heart to stomach war. The heavens finger them for shame and shower them with dust be swirl and maze! Sickness be their souls. Even now their numbers shrink and scatter! They rush to join our side. We welcome them! Others back and hide in holes and cover in brush. Dreggies rise! The time is now! The world be ARZ for the taking! Stand and hold with head to sky! They cannot last the night.

[Jazz rises and falls; continues soft under]

A2: Freedom waits the morning light. Strange daze and melancholy fever settles with the storm. Jazz be blue in B flat minor.
A1: The end of the Underground is at hand. More than mourning strikes the soul and buries us in blue and clouded

skies. Be the Dark One works her magic still?

A2: She works her magic on the field of war. Our brave be crouch and cringe before her grit and mettle. Valor be her shield. She drives the tunnel to death's core 'til bulldog guts and daring pull her up again. Praise be glory to the Dark One! This victory be hers!

A1: (listless) Praise be glory but the line be draw and mark in stone. Dark be Righteous whore.

A2: Was, A1, no more.

A1: What tune is this? Brain back the time and brother be alive!

A2: I brain, sage and take it to the core. Still jazz be blues and blues again. The downer the down and downer more.

A1: She be warn and heed. D'Arc be no man's fool and has no need to rule in peace the Dregs she leads in war. She be long gone and far away when tomorrow meets today.

A2: She brains no back and save herself. When sure and without doubt be victory, she stands before you and greets her destiny ball to ball. She will not run away.

A1: Then D'Arc must fall! Word be word. Dregs blood be on her hands. Righteous cash be line her leathered hide. She plays me for a fool in major chord.

A2: We play ourselves and diddle dumb. The greater fool be I whose brother's blood still settles in his veins.

A1: What would you have me do? Turn and fade away? Do nothing? Say nothing? Whatever Darkness does be cool blue ocean breeze? Scumbag rule be mock and cower with disease! It cannot be!

A2: We do what we must do. Say what we must say. Feel what we must feel. Glory be not praise for strange daze be ARZ. Give me leave, A1, to brain behind and sage what is to come.

A1: Chill, A2, and cool breeze go with you. Freedom be praise and glory enough for Dregs who find the light of newborn day.

A2: I fear. Freedom without D'Arc be stutter step and stumble. Chill and prosper.

[Doors open, close; exit A2]

A1: He marks my push and pull most deadly. Without the Dark One freedom be a dream without wings. Dreggies be underground ever always. Scumbag rule be echo in the void. Jazz be down, downer and flat. Heart be stern, sturdy and stone. D'Arc be traitor. She plays both sides against the core and jumps aboard the victory parade! What care am I she burns? Let her rise and she will raise the Rez and dump the Scumbags lickety split who brain too much her dark secret. Scumbags fall and Scumbag word be hollow chord of vengeance and destroy. Give her a pinch and she will squirm and wriggle free to burn the hand that pardons. D'Arc must fly or die or cause and A1 wonder kind be lost. But how will Dreggies bounce to this beat? She moves even he whose brother falls by her embrace. If I could drive the stars as she does I'd bid them drive her far, far away. But if she stays to face this dragon, jazz be nimble, brain be quick, D'Arc must choose her fate and I must make it stick!

[Gong and jazz, rise and fade; flurry as D'ARC appears]

CHORUS XV

D'ARC: Day be done and battle won! The war be victory!

A1: (solemn) Praise and glory!

D'ARC: Praise and glory behind. Ball to ball, heart to heart, I come to face the charge and drag it down or die. Truth be glory and justice be the call.

A1: Take the platform, Dark One. Beeps, Rez and Scumbags all must ear this trial to brainsage what must be done. Speak and make account.

D'ARC: Scumbags, Beeps and Rez! Dreggies all and everywhere! Darkness brings you praise and glory! Victory and peace be ARZ! Throw down your guard and breathe new air in freedom! (pause) But pause your rightful revelry and heed my call. I stand before you proud and without tremor, a warrior wronged and much abused by hands that stand before me not and have no names or faces.

A1: The Righteous be Nogo in the sacred Underground.

D'ARC: Who fingers me a traitor?

A1: The Righteous tower techs who fear no doom before them and claim you as their friend.

D'ARC: I have no friends but those who shoulder me in battle and share the call.

A1: Comrades then. They serve the Tower Lords and take their pay before the fall.

D'ARC: Truth be part and parcel...but not all.

A1: Mark it, post and save: Reverse your brain in time. The high goes flat and D'Arc appears, a leathered hag with sacred seed to raise the fallen offering. How now, D'Arc? Bitch be witch or something smells?

D'ARC: Witches burn in hell, in heaven fly!

A1: To the light! And darkness is no more!

D'ARC: The Righteous sent before me feed your weed with Nogo to the high. They line my leathers with sacred seed to warm you to my cause.

A1: The Righteous sent before the lead: Then sacred seed goes flat! How now?

D'ARC: The Tower Lords finger me a traitor right and true and move to put the stopper on my rise. Too late.

A1: Jazz be turn and turn again! They say she serves herself that serves the winning side! How now the voices that only Darkness hears?

D'ARC: Voices be real and heaven sent! They serve the cause of just!

A1: Who brains what voices serve? If voices turn and back the Righteous be return, what then be Dark One's move?

D'ARC: The voices would not, could not back the Righteous cause.

A1: Chill not, will not answer! She trembles at the thought! Voices be the cause of D'Arc, not just!

D'ARC: Brain, sage and take it to heart: The voices lead us to the triumph of this day! Just be trust and praise the newborn free! If voices bid me jump the moon then jump the moon I would and heart the cause be right and true!

A1: Freeze and back you to the part and parcel truth: Who bid you join the Righteous Ones and serve the Tower Lords?

D'ARC: The voices guide me ever always.

A1: Did you hold to brain the cause of just? Or praise and glory be blind trust?

D'ARC: (pause) Faith be blind that follows darkness into heaven's light. The voices be the cause! No other cause be mine.

A1: Balls be open and sage no trust where lead be blind. (pause) She falls silent and trance-like rides the wind of contemplation.

D'ARC: I have no more words to calm and comfort you. I pledge no oath to Scum nor Beep nor Rez nor any cause belonging to a man! My heart, my soul, my spirit all belong to heaven whose voices own and speak my will!

A1: Jazz be murder in cold, cold blood. How now?

D'ARC: Righteous blood be need to pave the path of just.

A1: Blood be not Righteous but Underground true blue and trickle down to serve the cause of just.

D'ARC: My heart mourns as yours for the brother of A2.

A1: But not as much as his, I sage. How now, Dark One? Who gives the knowing of this deed? Not I, not A2, we hold it back for knowing not. Then who?

D'ARC: The Righteous line was then still mine and open to my ears.

A1: She brains the deed before its doing but raises not the stopper? Wise be the whys. Did she brainsage the message: D'Arc be Righteous whore?

D'ARC: (pause) The message was within my knowing. Wise be the why that questions my not doing. The question burns without the asking. Could I have saved him? Yes, I sage. But the cause be all and stopper would have been my fall. Wrong, I sage. Guilt and sorrow follow.

A1: Jazz be move and suffer. Set you now in my place. D'Arc gives us knowing of deceit and Righteous lies that moved her to our door. She takes no oath and claims no loyalty to Dregs or cause of just. She takes the blood of Underground true blue upon her hands. What fate am I to serve?

D'ARC: (pause) Jazz be destiny. Burn baby burn! The Darkness mounts the stake and bury me in holy flame! Jazz be mourn and sorrow. I fall and ashes rise to heaven! Sacrifice and sainthood. Martyr be my name. Shake and shudder not before the gate! Embrace it! I have no shame.

A1: Chill to the marrow. Heart be sick and sorrow be the dawn of no tomorrow! Mark it post and save: D'Arc chooses fate and calls the flame of holy light! She burns by her own hand.

[Dark jazz, down and downer]

CHORUS XVI
(Jazz under)

[Gong: doors open and close as A2 enters]

A2: Hold and chill, A1! Roll back the time and stay your judgment! Proof positive be mine, palm and fist! The tower techs that talk and talk again, both sides against the core. They fear the Tower Lords return and finger D'Arc for shelter. Now fear no more they speak the whole and upper truth! The Dark One has no blame and wears none but Righteous blood upon her robes! The Tower Lords be plot and plan to kill the messenger and mark the Dark be burn baby burn! D'Arc storms the Righteous Guard when deadly deed be done. She could not put the stopper as she fears in guilt and sorrow. Blame not, shame not. Lay not my brother's death at Dark One's door. He died that she could win this war. Praise and glory! D'Arc be Queen of everything and everything she touches turn to gold! Time be peace and revelry! Let Darkness lead the way!

A1: Praise and glory! Let it be so. Pardon be D'Arc for crime be not hers. For though she burns me much and many ways I have no want to stain the ocean breeze with scorched leather. Jazz be peace and revelry! Praise be glory to the Dark and only Warrior Queen!

[Gong and scat jazz rise and fall]

A1: We are the scum that crawls out of the cracks in America's nightmare!
A2: We are the byproducts of industrial rage!
D'ARC: We are the residue of hazardous waste!
A1: We are the dregs of the technologic age!

[Jazz flurry, fades under]

D'ARC: And the Dregs inherit the earth! Even now the Army of the Underground grows by leap and bound! We streak to tower after tower 'til all be fall and Lords be Lords no more! The Righteous Guard be torn and ever always scatter! The Tower Lords plead for mercy and offer up their arms. Righteous tyranny be banish and vanish with the tide! The earth be ARZ in clay to make again in wisdom and in faith.

A2: The order of the day be bold and new and free!

A1: And Darkness leads to light!

A2: The Dark One watches over us and warns all unbelievers!

D'ARC: My eyes are always everywhere! We will not suffer traitors to the cause of just! Mark it and take heed!

A1: Food for hunger free of charge!

D'ARC: Come to the towers and help us organize the growing and the giving.

A1: Jobs for all who call and ones that suit your substance and device. Dregs be colorblind!

A2: Laser stun be ban and done! No more to burn submission!

D'ARC: Boundaries drop and guards report for honest living!

A1: Free travel to all and everywhere! The land be ARZ to roam where heart desire!

A2: Righteous Guard be hold and stop! Come join the army to feed the poor!

D'ARC: Access to the stars! Explore the heavens with our blessings!

A1: Homes be plenty of decent make! The homeless be no more!

A2: The sacred root and seed and sacred weed be legalize and free! Your bodies and your souls be yours to please!

D'ARC: Airwaves and interwaves be open to all! Teach your brothers and sisters! Feed your minds!

A1: These be the order of the newborn day! Brain back and save: The seed, root and origin of cause! Slate be clean! Nogo to the blame! Nada to the shame! All be equal and free! No crimes before this day! Voices be praise! The new age begins today!

D'ARC: Sage and glory! May the voices guide you ever always!

[Gong and scat jazz rise and fall]

Narrator: It is written. The time is past that is the future. The Underground Rebellion succeeds and covers the earth with peace, freedom and justice. The age of enlightenment begins. Jazz, art and creativity flourish. The universe of humankind expands. Spirit worlds open and are embraced. Tolerance is unnecessary. A thousand years of peace.

[Jazz flurry rises and fades.]

END ACT TWO.

FOSDICK & MULDOON

(The Continuing Story)

SETTING

The living quarters of Muldoon's suburban home. A couch and two chairs surround a coffee table. There is a bar upstage right, a library and writing desk stage left. The entry is down right. The furnishings are plain and comfortable. There is significant clutter. The time is now and the action is continuous.

CHARACTERS

MULDOON: A middle-aged writer.
FOSDICK: Younger than Muldoon, a devoted game player.
SADIE: A hard attractive woman, beginning to lose her youthful beauty.
EMERSON: A middle-aged accountant.
BESS: Emerson's seemingly simple-minded wife.

Fosdick and Muldoon was originally staged at Johnny Miller's Uptown Arena in Modesto, California, with the following cast:

> MULDOON: Scott Raven
> FOSDICK: Ray Miller
> SADIE: Shelley Weir
> EMERSON: Michael David Caine
> BESS: Gail Beebe

ACT ONE

[MULDOON enters from the upstage door carrying a well-worn folder, scattering papers in his wake. He crosses down center to the couch, placing the folder on the coffee table. He lights a cigarette and takes a long drag. He places it in a full ashtray and begins leafing through the folder, stopping at a particular page and reads...]

MULDOON: "And so I am reduced to this: That I can think of no meaning that justifies this passing, that I can perceive not a hint at the purpose of this existence." Hmm. Garbage. Nothing but garbage. [rises, crosses to his desk stage left] At least, I hope it is.

[He places the folder on the desk and walks to the bar upstage left. He prepares two drinks, leaves one at the bar and returns to the couch. He sets his drink down, props his feet on the coffee table and leans back, giving the appearance of deep thought. He takes another drag.]

I wonder what Mother Nature intended the human race to think of itself when she gave us the same organs to piss and procreate with. I just wonder.

[FOSDICK knocks on the door stage right. MULDOON sighs and answers it.]

FOSDICK: Hello, my name is...
MULDOON: Fosdick. I'm Muldoon. [extends his hand, FOSDICK shakes; MULDOON crosses to the bar] If you can believe that. At last we meet.

[FOSDICK enters, confused]

FOSDICK: How would you...? What do you mean, at last...?

MULDOON: Please come in. Feel at home. Have a drink. [hands him one] In fact, have two. [hands him the second, closes the door and returns to take a drink] Well?

FOSDICK: I uh...thanks.

MULDOON: Certainly. It compliments the occasion, don't you think?

FOSDICK: I suppose.

MULDOON: Of course. Less demanding. Supposition that is. As opposed to thoughtfulness. Where were we? Oh yes, you were just saying: How would you? How would you? How would I what? [FOSDICK starts to answer] No, no, let me guess.

FOSDICK: If you insist.

MULDOON: Insist? Of course I insist. I do have my standards. [pacing] How would I? How would I what? How would I know! That's it, isn't it? How would I know what? How would I know your name? Fosdick? Well, that's simple enough. That high brow, those squinty eyes, that protruding nose and those jowls – my God, they look like misplaced goiters! Fosdick, you frankly look like a Fosdick.

FOSDICK: There's a problem, Muldoon – if that is in fact your name. I don't have jowls or squinty eyes or...

MULDOON: Are you sure? [examines his face] I suppose you're right for the most part. But then that's not how I knew your name, Fosdick. "At last?" Did you say, "At last?"

FOSDICK: No, you said "at last."

MULDOON: When?

FOSDICK: Just now.

MULDOON: Just now?

FOSDICK: A moment ago. At the door. You said, "At

last we meet."

MULDOON: And so we do. I'm Muldoon. Pleased...
FOSDICK: I know.
MULDOON: ...to meet you. You know? You know that I'm pleased?
FOSDICK: No. I know that you're Muldoon. Or at least you say...
MULDOON: How would you know that?
FOSDICK: [smiles] Simple, that round, pudgy face, that bulbous nose, the empty forlorn gaze. Frankly, Muldoon, you simply look like a Muldoon.
MULDOON: Thank you, Fosdick.

[MULDOON crosses to sit in his chair, stage left of the coffee table.]

FOSDICK: Cartoon characters, weren't they?
MULDOON: Who?
FOSDICK: Fosdick and Muldoon. Fearless Fosdick, I believe it was.
MULDOON: I wouldn't know.
FOSDICK: Wouldn't you?
MULDOON: You're not questioning my originality, are you, Fosdick?
FOSDICK: [sitting opposite Muldoon] Not at all. After all, I believe there is such a thing as original plagiarism. It has everything to do with context. In fact, I would venture to say that a borrowed phrase or idea may be more creative than the original.
MULDOON: Please sit down.
FOSDICK: I am sitting. Thank you.
MULDOON: So you are. So you are. What brings you here, Mr. Fosdick?
FOSDICK: Well, it concerns your dog.
MULDOON: Emerson?

FOSDICK: Emerson?

MULDOON: As in Ralph Waldo.

FOSDICK: Yes. Well, you see, I ride a bicycle to work.

MULDOON: Environmentally conscious. Commendable. Responsible.

FOSDICK: I do what I can. We should all do what we can. It's also economical. In any case, as I do ride my bicycle to work every day and as my route invariably takes me by your house twice a day, I've had several rather unsettling encounters with your dog.

MULDOON: Emerson.

FOSDICK: This is a serious matter.

MULDOON: Is it? Yes. Emerson is a very serious dog.

FOSDICK: I do hope you're not taking this lightly.

MULDOON: Believe me, I'm taking it quite as serious as you are. It's my nature to take things seriously.

FOSDICK: The fact is your dog...

MULDOON: Emerson.

FOSDICK: Emerson attacked me.

MULDOON: You're very concerned with the facts, aren't you?

FOSDICK: As a matter of fact I am.

MULDOON: Would you like to talk about it?

FOSDICK: Not just now, thank you.

MULDOON: No bother. Any time. You'll let me know?

FOSDICK: I don't think you understand.

MULDOON: Really? Have I missed something?

FOSDICK: I think you may have. When I say your dog...

MULDOON: Emerson.

FOSDICK: [anger building] When I say your dog ... [MULDOON raises his hand] ... Emerson attacked me, I mean that literally.

MULDOON: As opposed to metaphorically?

FOSDICK: Not once, mind you, and not twice but three

times. And I'm not referring to a little "run and peck" nip at the foot. I really wouldn't have minded. It comes with the territory. But your dog... Emerson burst from behind your rosebushes, knocked me to the ground, tore my suit and opened a wound that required seventeen stitches.

MULDOON: My Emerson?

FOSDICK: It is you dog, isn't it?

MULDOON: Emerson is hardly larger than a football.

FOSDICK: I realize that. Nevertheless.

MULDOON: Impressive, really. Don't you think?

FOSDICK: I suppose. Nevertheless.

MULDOON: What did you do?

FOSDICK: What do you mean?

MULDOON: You've told me what my little dog did. What did you do? It goes against Emerson's nature to attack an innocent bystander without provocation.

FOSDICK: You're suggesting I provoked...

MULDOON: I'm suggesting we've only heard half of the story. Unfortunately, Emerson can't very well speak for himself.

FOSDICK: I could have called the pound. I could sue you for God's sake!

MULDOON: Please, let's not invoke the deity.

FOSDICK: All right. Let's be reasonable. Why would I provoke your dog?

MULDOON: Emerson.

FOSDICK: Emerson.

MULDOON: It's puzzling but take a fresh look at it from my perspective. Why should I take your word against a long-time friend and loyal companion? To the best of my awareness, Emerson bears no ill will to any being on the planet. Then there's you: A stranger who enters my home, defiles my dog and threatens to sue me should I not concede and make restitution. What would you have me do? Lock the little creature up? Chain him to a stake? Or would nothing short of execution satisfy your need for ... justice?

FOSDICK: I didn't expect...

MULDOON: I didn't ask what you didn't expect.

FOSDICK: All right then. I thought you might confine him during the day.

MULDOON: Lock him up?

FOSDICK: That's right. You could keep him inside.

MULDOON: There are indoor dogs and outdoor dogs. Emerson is no pup. Lock him up and you might as well shoot him.

FOSDICK: The alternative...is not pleasant.

MULDOON: You're heartless, Fosdick.

FOSDICK: On the contrary I think I've shown great latitude and compassion under the circumstances.

MULDOON: Do you?

FOSDICK: I do. Given the alternative, locking the little monster up is a generous solution I should think.

MULDOON: You should. More often and with greater depth. May I be frank?

FOSDICK (smiling): You can be anyone you'd like.

MULDOON: You're not really interested in my dog.

FOSDICK: I'm not?

MULDOON: You're better than that, Fosdick. Emerson is just a dog. Rule number one: When I call your bluff, you throw in your cards. Got it?

FOSDICK: Got what? A rule to what? Are we playing a game?

MULDOON: Of course. That's why you're here. A game, a match, a showdown, a duel. I'm challenging you to a duel.

FOSDICK: Let me get this straight. You're challenging me to a game?

MULDOON: Yes.

FOSDICK: I'm curious. What kind of game?

MULDOON: A civilized game. You're already familiar with the rules. The object of this game, this match, this dual over the dog, is to rip your opponent to shreds, to utterly destroy him without exposing your talons, your fangs, for if you do you make yourself vulnerable. You expose yourself to the harshest criticism society can dole out. That in turn destroys you. You can lie and cheat and deceive but if you're caught...

FOSDICK: You throw in your cards.

MULDOON: That's right, Fosdick. You're a fast learner. Shall we get under way?

FOSDICK: What makes you think I'm the sort of person who would engage in your little game?

MULDOON: You will because it's in your nature. You will because you're exactly the kind of person who likes to play little games. You're a conflict-oriented businessman who thrives on the daily kill and would do virtually anything for the taste of fresh blood and the thrill of a virgin conquest. You will because I've issued a challenge and you think of yourself as a man who will not turn his back on a challenge. You will because...I would very much like you to leave.

FOSDICK: Is that right?

MULDOON: That's right.

FOSDICK: I should walk out right now and leave you wallowing in your own misery.

MULDOON: You should.

FOSDICK: I should.

MULDOON: But you won't.

FOSDICK: Why not?

MULDOON: It's simple, Fosdick. You've already stayed too long. If you walk out now, you've conceded. You've lost the game. And if you lose it means I'm right about you. The winner is always right. It's the winner's right to be right. And if I'm right about you then you're a very ugly person, Fosdick. Heartless, vindictive and broadly unworthy of the blessings this life bestows on you. Face it, Fosdick, you leave now and you're stuck with the truth for the rest of your miserable existence.

FOSDICK: I don't believe that will be necessary.

MULDOON: Don't you?

FOSDICK: I accept the challenge.

MULDOON: I thought you might.

FOSDICK: I do. But not for the reasons you've given. You see, Muldoon, I've heard about your little charades. I sought you out. I've been looking forward to this.

MULDOON: Then the whole dog story was a bluff?

FOSDICK: Seriously, do I look like I ride a bike?

MULDOON: Congratulations. I underestimated you.

FOSDICK: Thank you.

MULDOON: I won't do it again.

FOSDICK: Are you sure?

MULDOON: But don't you see, Fosdick, it confirms my theory.

FOSDICK: What theory? You have a theory?

MULDOON: I have many. This one concerns the nature of humankind. More specifically, mankind as represented by one of its more revered members: A successful businessman, husband and father, a pillar of the Chamber of Commerce community. Namely: you, Fosdick.

FOSDICK: I'm flattered. Out of a myriad of possibilities, you chose me to represent humanity.

MULDOON: Apparently you volunteered.

FOSDICK: There are no accidents.

MULDOON: Are there not?

FOSDICK: I don't think so but that's not the point. I'd like to know more about your theory of mankind.

MULDOON: I'd be content to oblige you if I had the time.

FOSDICK: You have all the time in the world.

MULDOON: Really. How would you know? In any case my theory of humanity would require volumes to be analyzed and synthesized by dozens of elite experts in psychology, sociology and neurology. It is beyond your limited ability to comprehend.

FOSDICK: I'll be the judge of that.

MULDOON: Hardly. But allow me to summarize: Bloated to absurd proportions by a false sense of his own importance, man has become an empty vessel on a meaningless voyage to his own doom. His values are reduced to a scrapheap of rusted technology. His institutions are guarded shelters for the greedy and corrupt. His sense of duty to and responsibility for his fellow humans begins and ends with his own aggrandizement.

FOSDICK: That's your abridged version?

MULDOON: For the moment.

FOSDICK: Where's the data? How have you confirmed your theory?

MULDOON: You're here, aren't you? You sought me out. Why?

FOSDICK: Must you always repeat yourself?

MULDOON: It's in my nature.

FOSDICK: It should be against the rules.

MULDOON: What? Repetition?

FOSDICK: No, rationalization.

MULDOON: Not at all but when you're caught…

FOSDICK: You're caught.

MULDOON: You throw in your cards.

FOSDICK: Have we started?

MULDOON: Had we stopped?

FOSDICK: That's makes us even.

MULDOON: Even?

FOSDICK: The score. One to one. We're even.

MULDOON: Don't be absurd. There is no score. And I was just beginning to regard you with a modicum of respect.

FOSDICK: What? There is no score?

MULDOON: What purpose would it serve?

FOSDICK: Traditionally, it determines the winner.

MULDOON: You actually believe that?

FOSDICK: Of course. It's normal. If you get the most points, score the most runs, kick the most goals or gather the most tokens, whatever the game, you win!

MULDOON: This is no child's game. This is real and we both know how it works.

FOSDICK: House rules?

MULDOON: Always.

FOSDICK: All right. So you tell me, Muldoon, how does it work?

MULDOON: As if you don't know.

FOSDICK: For the record. So there's no confusion.

MULDOON: For the record, then, there is but one path to victory. There is but one manner of defeat. Victory is by concession only. If there is no concession, there is no victory.

FOSDICK: So one of us has to concede?

MULDOON: Yes.

FOSDICK: Concede to what?

MULDOON: Not what, whom. You will concede to me.

FOSDICK: Or you to me.

MULDOON: Not likely. [crosses to the bar, prepares three drinks] Meantime, we're expecting guests. They'll be here momentarily.

FOSDICK: [smiles] So you've invited your friends.

MULDOON: Guests, Fosdick, guests.

FOSDICK: Can I assume they'll be playing this little game of yours as well?

MULDOON: You can assume anything you like.

FOSDICK: I assume you're fixing the game.

MULDOON: We need people, Fosdick. We need potential allies and enemies with their own interests and their own agendas. Pieces on a chessboard. The single quality that connects them is that they're all willing to play.

[A knock on the door, party sounds; MULDOON answers.]

MULDOON: Our guests have arrived! Greetings! [the guests enter] Fosdick, meet Sadie, Bess and ... Emerson.
FOSDICK: Emerson?
MULDOON: Emerson. Sadie, Bess, Emerson, meet Fosdick. Well, actually it's Peter or Fred or something equally mundane but he prefers to be called Fosdick. Silly of him, isn't it?
BESS: [giggles; to Emerson] Oh, he's kidding. Isn't he kidding?
EMERSON: Of course he is, dear. [they shake hands] Pleased to meet you.
BESS: Yes, pleased.
SADIE: [edging by, sitting] The same, I'm sure.

[MULDOON gestures, they all sit.]

MULDOON: And Fosdick is very pleased to meet you. Aren't you, Fosdick?
FOSDICK: Of course.
MULDOON: Of course he is. Sadie, you look in need of a drink.
SADIE: Have you got one?
MULDOON: I do. Fosdick?
FOSDICK: Yes?
MULDOON: Could you serve, please?
FOSDICK: Sure. [crosses to bar]
MULDOON: Actually he's my new domestic.
FOSDICK: Foul, Muldoon.
EMERSON: Muldoon?
MULDOON: Muldoon. You see, Fosdick and I are playing a little game.
SADIE: Tell me something I don't know.
MULDOON: We were about to ask you to join us.
FOSDICK: If you'd like to, of course.

MULDOON: Of course.

BESS: [stands] Oh good! I like games!

SADIE: I hate games but if that's what it takes to qualify for the bar, I'm in.

MULDOON: That's the spirit. There are plenty of spirits for active participants. And you, Emerson?

EMERSON: Absolutely! I enjoy a good game.

MULDOON: Excellent. Now Fosdick will get another chance.

EMERSON: Another chance at what?

MULDOON: Defeating you.

EMERSON: Really? [to Fosdick] So you're saying I've defeated you in the past?

MULDOON: Fosdick would never concede to that, would you, Fosdick?

FOSDICK: Not at all. [to Emerson] I assure you we've never met.

MULDOON: That's not what you told me.

FOSDICK: That was another Emerson.

MULDOON: You're sure?

FOSDICK: Sure as sweat on a summer day.

MULDOON: Which Emerson was it?

FOSDICK: Just some other Emerson. It doesn't matter.

MULDOON: Emerson Smith? Emerson Jones?

FOSDICK: Emerson Dean I believe it was.

MULDOON: [to Emerson] Then it was you!

EMERSON: Indeed!

FOSDICK: Small world, isn't it?

EMERSON: So what was it: golf, tennis, pool?

FOSDICK: I believe it was...wrestling.

EMERSON: Sure, sure, weren't you that kid from Washington Heights?

SADIE: That was me and I kicked your ass.

FOSDICK: [laughs] That's one for Sadie for those who keep score.

BESS: Oh, have we started?

FOSDICK: Had we stopped?

BESS: But what do we do?

SADIE: Stay out of it, dear, and count your blessings.

BESS: That's no fun.

MULDOON: Bess is right. You have to play to have fun and if you don't play you might lose your friends. No one likes a wallflower. Do we, Fosdick?

FOSDICK: We do not.

MULDOON: You see? Fosdick would begin to distance himself. After a while even Bess might begin to wonder.

BESS: [laughs, transitions to serious] Oh, he's kidding.

MULDOON: That's right, Bess. I'm a great joker. It's part of my nature. Nevertheless, your part...

SADIE: Should she choose to accept it...

MULDOON: That's right. We believe in free choice, don't we, Fosdick?

FOSDICK: We do.

MULDOON: Your parts, ladies and gentleman, should you choose to accept them, is simply to take sides.

BESS: Oh, that's easy.

EMERSON: One question: How do you win a game like that?

MULDOON: From your perspective?

EMERSON: Yes, it's only one I've got.

MULDOON: By being on the winning side.

EMERSON: Fair enough. Can we switch?

MULDOON: Yes.

EMERSON: At any time?

MULDOON: At any time.

EMERSON: Offhand it sounds a little simple.

SADIE: It sounds cold blooded.

MULDOON: I'm afraid Sadie's right. But it's more fun that way, right Bess?

BESS: Oh. (as in: Oh, he's kidding)

FOSDICK: If you want to make fun of someone,

Muldoon, aim it at me. Bess doesn't deserve your belligerence.

BESS: Don't be upset. He's just kidding.

FOSDICK: You think so? Ask him. Call his bluff.

EMERSON: Look, if anyone's getting belligerent here it's you. You have to learn when to take things seriously and when not to.

MULDOON: Very good, Emerson. It may well be the game is too easy for a man of your capabilities. Play your cards right and you may get a more challenging role next time around. That's how it works. Right, Bess?

BESS: I should think so.

MULDOON: You should but what you actually think is: Why can't we play a more civilized game like charades. Would you like to play charades, my dear?

BESS: Oh yes, I love charades.

MULDOON: I bet you do.

EMERSON: Careful, Muldoon, there's a fine line between innocent fun and rudeness.

MULDOON: Have I crossed it yet?

EMERSON: I believe you're approaching it.

MULDOON: Stand aside, my friend, I'm about to plough through. [to Bess] Do you know what the biggest charade of all is? Do you, my dear?

BESS: I'm sure I don't know what you mean.

MULDOON: Of course you don't but I'm about to tell you. How would that be? Would you like to know? Would you like to know what the biggest charade of all is?

BESS: I suppose.

MULDOON: Your marriage.

EMERSON: That's enough!

MULDOON: Have I crossed the line?

EMERSON: You have.

MULDOON: Have I achieved outright belligerence?

EMERSON: I would say you're downright...

MULDOON: I should have thought up left. You see, I

imagine an audience there (points). But you say I'm down right? That means the audience is there (points). It exposes my weak side. We can't have that.

EMERSON: Can't we?

MULDOON: No, we cannot.

SADIE: That assumes you have a strong side.

MULDOON: Now who's being belligerent?

SADIE: I'm belligerent, you're belligerent, he's belligerent, we're all belligerent except Bess. So what?

BESS: I can be belligerent, too.

EMERSON: Sure, Bess.

BESS: I can. If you don't think so it's because you don't think.

EMERSON: Fine, Bess, you're belligerent, too.

BESS: I'm not but I can be.

FOSDICK: Look, either you're belligerent or you're not. You can't have it both ways.

EMERSON: She can if she wants.

BESS: I'm not belligerent but I can be. What's wrong with that?

SADIE: She has a point.

MULDOON: Of course she does. She has a point, you have a point, we all have a point. The real question is: Is it in her nature? I admit Bess is a difficult case. Her true nature may be suppressed. A charade if you will. Whereas Fosdick here is a brilliant shining example of absolute belligerence.

FOSDICK: If mine shines, Muldoon, yours radiates.

MULDOON: Brilliant, Fosdick, brilliant.

EMERSON: I'd say Mr. Fosdick has a point.

SADIE: He has, she has, we all have. Mine is to make it to the next drink. [standing] Mind if I...?

MULDOON: Be my guest.

FOSDICK: She is your guest. Do you mind...?

MULDOON: Not at all.

[Silence while SADIE fixes her drink.]

SADIE: What is this, a funeral?

MULDOON: We do seem to be in a lull.

SADIE: Rush hour traffic in Holland Tunnel moves faster than this. What's the matter, kids? Lost that fun loving, game playing spirit? Or are we plotting our next moves? Preparing the next attack?

EMERSON: Get off it, Sadie.

SADIE: Get off what, Emerson? I'm not on anything. That is one of my myriad problems.

FOSDICK: If you don't mind my asking, Sadie, why are you so cynical?

SADIE: I do actually.

FOSDICK: You're a very attractive woman. You're witty and obviously intelligent.

SADIE: Are you making a play, Fos*dick*?

FOSDICK: I imagine you could be quite charming if you applied your talents more constructively.

SADIE: How do you mean, constructively? Do you think I could be more successful like you? Or maybe I could find a good, reliable husband like Emerson. Is that what you mean?

EMERSON: What he means, if I may, is that you would be quite a catch for some lucky man if you weren't so negative. You can match wits with anyone but instead of connecting with people, you spout your one-liners, get drunk and end up being left out.

SADIE: So I'm being left out? What a shame! Left out of what? Trivial arguments about trivial lives? So much of nothing and what it really comes down to is ego, doesn't it? Well, I won't feed yours and I'm not interested in feeding my own so what exactly am I missing?

FOSDICK: In a word: life. If you avoid conflict you're missing everything. You're left out of life itself.

RANDOM PLAYS

SADIE: I see. So conflict is a necessary commodity like air and water. True in the movies, honey, not in life. You can fool yourself all you want. I'm not buying it.

FOSDICK: So we all float through life without ever bumping into each other. Who's fooling themselves? A world without problems to fight through, without people who oppose us, without barriers to overcome, would be boring as hell.

MULDOON: That's a gem, Fosdick. Did you think it up all by yourself or did you pick it up from last night's late show? People don't bump into each other by chance. People aren't problems to be overcome. People don't oppose us by accident. When a problem arises you can be sure someone created it. When a conflict presents itself, it was welcomed. It was desired. It was plotted, planned and executed. We spend so much of our time trying to justify and rationalize that part of ourselves that craves drama. That ugly, despicable part of ourselves that yearns for nothing more than to devour our fellow beings. [to the group] Say, did you ever hear the story of the dog and the man on a bicycle? Well, the dog attacked the man on the bicycle. Literally and ferociously attacked the man. The man did not shy away. He did not attempt to avoid the beast. He stubbornly refused to alter his route and came back again and again. Not once but three times. Count them: One, two, three.

[BESS counts on her fingers, giggles]

Once. It happens. An unfortunate but isolated incident. Twice. Tenacity. Curiosity maybe. Three times? You wanted it. You welcomed it. You dreamed of it and you got it. Fosdick, you fool, you willed that dog to bite you!

SADIE: What the hell are you talking about?

MULDOON: I'm defending you, Sadie. Can't you tell? I'm protecting you from these carnivorous wimps who only moments ago were at each other's throats. The moment someone threatens their precious little game they're playing doubles side by side.

SADIE: Fuck off, Mac. I don't need protection. But thanks for the sentiment. Now what was it about the dog and the man on a bicycle?

MULDOON: It was about Emerson.

SADIE: Emerson?

MULDOON: Emerson and Fosdick.

EMERSON: Fosdick and I?

MULDOON: Emerson Dean. Isn't that right, Fosdick?

FOSDICK: Emerson is a dog.

EMERSON: Which Emerson is that?

FOSDICK: Emerson Dean, I said.

EMERSON: I'm not sure how to take that.

FOSDICK: Don't take it at all, idiot.

BESS: Oh, he's just kidding, dear. Everyone's kidding. It's just a game.

EMERSON: Well, I know that and I'm just playing along but...

BESS: Now, now, don't start.

EMERSON: Don't start? When did we stop?

BESS: I'm stopping now. Sadie's right. I'm tired of playing.

MULDOON: Good for you, Bess. Assert yourself!

BESS: I quit. I'm not playing anymore.

MULDOON: I'm with you. Bess and I refuse to play.

EMERSON: You pushed her into it, Muldoon.

MULDOON: I did? When?

EMERSON: Just now.

MULDOON: Just now?

EMERSON: You prodded her.

MULDOON: [to Bess] Do you quit or don't you?

BESS: I quit!

MULDOON: She quits! I quit! That's it, children.

SADIE: If that means you don't have to play for drinks, I

quit too.

FOSDICK: All right, all right. [stands, walks around] So the game is over! Nobody wins, nobody loses. Fine. [waits] Look, Muldoon, if the game is over I've got no reason to be here, do I?

MULDOON: Without the game you have no reason to be.

FOSDICK: If you're quitting, I'm leaving. It's that simple.

MULDOON: But you're still here. What is it you want? A final tally? Sadie?

SADIE: I quit.

MULDOON: Bess?

BESS: I said I quit and I do.

MULDOON: Emerson?

EMERSON: [to Fosdick] At best that's three to two. We're outnumbered.

FOSDICK: All right. Okay. Fine. [prepares to leave; to Muldoon] Calling my bluff, are you? We'll see who's bluffing.

[FOSDICK exits]

MULDOON: Yes, we'll see. We'll see.

EMERSON: He really did. I'll be. I didn't think he had it in him.

MULDOON: Well, gang, what shall we do in the interim?

SADIE: I've got an idea. We drink ourselves to oblivion ...or death, whichever comes first.

EMERSON: Wait a minute. Something just happened here. Am I right? [chuckles] What exactly were you two playing?

MULDOON: Philosophical checkers.

EMERSON: Come on.

MULDOON: Doesn't appeal to you? How about psychological risk? Karmic pursuit? Trivial refutation?

EMERSON: Jesus, get serious.

MULDOON: What difference does it make? They're all the same.

EMERSON: I disagree. Every game has its own unique characteristics. Games of strategy, games of skill: the one requires tenacity, the other relies on instinct. The ability to make a sudden and unexpected move is essential. It makes all the difference. So this game of yours, Fosdick and Muldoon, what is the main idea?

MULDOON: The main idea?

EMERSON: The essential thrust, the primary motivation?

MULDOON: Well, to put it in terms you'll understand: You set out to destroy your opponent utterly and completely without exposing your claws, your fangs, that ugly vindictive part of who you are that you don't want the world to know about.

EMERSON: Claws?

MULDOON: You like it?

EMERSON: Very much.

MULDOON: I thought it might appeal to you.

EMERSON: It does. But if I may: What do you aim for?

MULDOON: [waits] I see. Strategy?

EMERSON: Yes. How do you go about it?

MULDOON: That's another question. Picking up pointers, are we? Auditioning for a future role? [EMERSON chuckles] To answer your first: You take aim at motive.

EMERSON: Motive?

MULDOON: Your opponent's belief system, core values, the thrust behind his or her actions.

EMERSON: So Fosdick was targeting your beliefs?

SADIE: Fosdick was wallowing in his own excrement.

He was targeting everything and nothing.

MULDOON: Correct on both accounts.

EMERSON: Fascinating. What do you believe in, Muldoon?

MULDOON: Like the lady implied: nothing.

SADIE: Did I say that?

BESS: Oh yes. Remember? You said...no, he said...well, you said something.

MULDOON: She said nothing – which is something I suppose.

EMERSON: That's a dodge, Muldoon. Everyone believes in something. You have to or you can't carry on.

MULDOON: I have believed in many things.

EMERSON: Aha! Now we're getting somewhere.

SADIE: Now we're getting nowhere at a slower pace.

MULDOON: Once again, the lady's right. There's no need to speak of the past.

EMERSON: To the contrary, the past is prelude. Besides, I'd like to know. Wouldn't you like to know, Bess?

BESS: Of course I would, dear.

EMERSON: You see? We're friends. We're interested in our friends. It's natural curiosity. So tell us: What did you believe in?

MULDOON: I suppose there's no harm in it.

SADIE: Masturbation is definitely harmless.

EMERSON: Bess and I are curious. That's all. We enjoy learning about our friends. Right, Bess?

BESS: Well, I think...

EMERSON: Now, now, Bess. Don't interrupt.

BESS: Oh, I'm sorry.

SADIE: You certainly are. Sorry, I couldn't resist.

MULDOON: You were not interrupting, I assure you.

BESS: No, no, you go on now. I'll be quiet. I'm not one to interrupt.

MULDOON: If you insist.

BESS: Of course I insist. I don't talk when my opinion is not wanted, even if I do have something to say. It's just that...
EMERSON: Bess?
BESS: Oh, I'm sorry. [giggles] You go on now.
MULDOON: Well, since you're interested...
SADIE: [standing, crossing to bar] I'll make myself another drink if you don't mind.
EMERSON: You're not interested?
MULDOON: She's heard it all before.
SADIE: It's the story of my life. [yawns]
EMERSON: In that case, I could use a refresher. Bess?
BESS: [spits up in the act of drinking, giggles, offers her glass] Please!
SADIE: I guess I'm the new domestic. [fixes drinks]
EMERSON: You were saying.
MULDOON: As I was saying, I once believed in many things. There was a time I even believed in other humans. I believed in the fundamental goodness of humankind. Once, I believed in a lady.
SADIE: A lady!
MULDOON: Yes, dear Sadie, a lady. Foolish of me, I know. Hopelessly naïve. But I would have given her anything. I'd have jumped Grand Canyon just to see her smile. Finally, one day, without any particular cause or reason, I realized that what I loved, what I valued and treasured more than life itself, was a fantasy. I imagined this perfect woman and cast her in the part. At the approximate same time, of course, she realized she'd be better off without this insecure, clownish fool shadowing her life, begging like a puppy on a leash for something that he could call love.
EMERSON: Reality can be brutal.
MULDOON: And so I quit believing in my beautiful lady. I could do that because I believed there were many beautiful ladies in the world.
EMERSON: There are, my friend. This world is

teeming with wonderful women and one of them…

BESS: Oh, is it?

EMERSON: I just meant…

MULDOON: No. It isn't. How lucky you are to have found just one. After a long period of dedicated pursuit, I could find no one. I gave up the search. I resolved to solitude and turned to the great issues of the world. At the time, we called it a revolution.

EMERSON: Free love, baby. Long live the revolution!

MULDOON: The revolution is dead.

SADIE: The revolution never dies; only the revolutionary.

MULDOON: Well, if the revolution isn't dead, it's in one hell of a slumber. Who knows? Maybe it was never born. What we called the revolution was built on a foundation of lies. Those who called themselves revolutionaries were mainly concerned with their own vanities. They used the great issues to feed their own publicity seeking egos. Not one could tell you what it all meant. Not one could elucidate what he or she believed was so critically important.

EMERSON: You stopped believing in the cause?

MULDOON: Not at first. I stopped believing in the people. Soon after I had to ask myself: What good is the cause without the people?

EMERSON: I see.

MULDOON: Do you?

EMERSON: More than you realize. So that was it? No more causes. No more love. No more faith.

MULDOON: Not quite. My faith in the external world was shaken. I shed my beliefs like a pair of jeans that no longer fit. I could do that because of one very important belief that I had somehow managed to hold on to through all the years of struggle. I believed I had something to say and I was more determined than ever to say it. In short, I still believed in myself.

SADIE: The day you give up believing in yourself is the day you cash in your chips. [examines him] We're not there, are we?

MULDOON: I can't say. And if I can't say I can't very well believe, can I? If I believe in nothing but myself how can I believe in myself? How can what I have to say have any real meaning? It's a conundrum, an impossible dilemma from which there is no escape. You see, Sadie, we're not so very different after all.

SADIE: The difference is: You're a writer. You have something to offer the world. You must still believe in your work. I do.

MULDOON: I've always placed ultimate value on my work, my art, the center of who I am. I still do. But the purpose was always to contribute something to the world, the great pool of human knowledge, the universe of thoughts and ideas that somehow, when combined with the ideas of others, would result in a better life for all. I now believe that the great pool of ideas is little more than a cesspool steeping in its own dung. My contributions? Was anyone listening? Was anyone reading? Even those who were made their own interpretations. They used my work to support their own distorted visions, to embellish their twisted tales. Games. Mundane, self-seeking, perverted games.

SADIE: You're not being fair. I've read your work. Of course I interpret it. If it ain't exactly what you meant, so what? Write it again. At least it inspires something. At least it makes me feel like I'm alive. Like I'm more than some mindless vermin crawling around in the gutter. At least I have something to interpret! That's something, isn't it?

MULDOON: It is. Something vague and uncertain and therefore unworthy as an object of faith. It is what it is.

SADIE: So now what?

MULDOON: Now I believe in nothing. [flashes a smile] Well folks, that's it!

RANDOM PLAYS

BESS: [applauds, giggles, applauds] Bravo! Bravo! Oh, that was wonderful! Even Sadie liked it. Didn't you, Sadie?

SADIE: No, Bess, I didn't like it. Not at all. There's just one more thing. I know it sounds ludicrous coming from me. It's not something I talk about. Neither do you. In all the time we've known each other, we've never brought it up. I'm bringing it up now: Did you ever believe in God?

EMERSON: [laughs] I'd sooner believe he is God than believe he ever believed in God.

MULDOON: [joins laughter] Yes, Sadie, I did. [laughter stops] Well, if not God exactly...

EMERSON: Aha!

MULDOON: ...then something like God. I believed in a God-like being, a divine presence if you will.

EMERSON: I don't believe it.

MULDOON: He doesn't believe it.

EMERSON: Not for a second.

MULDOON: You really need to get over this idea that if you don't believe something it isn't true. It might have been my greatest folly, I admit. I sometimes find it difficult to believe myself. But I did believe because I wanted to believe. I wanted the comfort of believing in something greater than myself. *When I was a child...* When I grew older I understood what a pack of mindless fools we all are. There's something truly frightening about a species capable of devoting itself to any sort of populist rot that comes along. It only requires an inspired voice to get the ball rolling.

SADIE: What religion are we talking about?

MULDOON: All religions but I was talking about people. Members of the human race who can believe in anything. Watch the good doctor cure little Johnny's incurable disease! Behold the politician with an answer to all our economic woes! Want a better sex life? Pop a pill, buy a car. Take two aspirin and call me in the morning. Buy me a drink, give me a dollar, because we care about you!

Anything! And for no other reason than they want to believe.

EMERSON: Very good, Muldoon. So you say you believe in nothing.

MULDOON: I believe in nothing. When a man believes in nothing what he says is irrelevant.

EMERSON: Very clever but you can't fool me.

BESS: Emerson!

EMERSON: Now dear, I know what I'm doing.

BESS: I know what you're doing, too, and you'd better stop. We stopped playing that game. Remember?

EMERSON: He hasn't stopped so it's fair game. Right, Muldoon?

MULDOON: Carry on.

EMERSON: I'm calling your bluff. Your story is too pat. I won't let you get away with it. That's the difference between me and Mr. Fosdick. You can fool him but you can't fool me.

MULDOON: No, I could never fool you.

EMERSON: [mocking] I don't believe in anything! [laughs] Good though. Very clever.

MULDOON: Not clever enough to get it past old Emerson though.

EMERSON: No, sir, I'm one step ahead of you.

BESS: [flash] Oh! He caught you!

SADIE: That's right, Bess. You're married to a real winner. Sad, isn't it?

MULDOON: You think it might work with Fosdick though?

EMERSON: I think it might. Now we'll never know.

MULDOON: Won't we?

EMERSON: He left.

MULDOON: Did he?

EMERSON: We all watched him leave!

BESS: Yes, I saw him. He walked out that door.

SADIE: What the man means is: He'll return.

EMERSON: Not a chance. You went too far. You

miscalculated. A man has to accept his mistakes.

MULDOON: He might be cleverer than you think. Maybe he's fooled you.

EMERSON: I'm telling you, he's gone.

MULDOON: We'll see. [glances at the clock] We still have a little time. What shall we do next?

EMERSON: Has anyone ever told you you're insane?

MULDOON: [eyes flare, deadly serious] Only once. You know, it's a funny thing about insanity. The insane can't stand to be called insane. It does things to them. Something dark takes hold of them. They can't control it.

[MULDOON grabs a fire poker resting conveniently nearby]

They want to...

[Breathing heavily he raises the poker with both hands]

They want to...viciously and indiscriminately...attack!

[He swings the poker violently down at Emerson, narrowly missing him and hitting the sofa. EMERSON jumps up and lands on the floor. He backs away and MULDOON pursues.]

A mad passion! An intense desire!

[He corners EMERSON against the wall]

A burning, raving, lunatic desire that cannot be suppressed until...

[Poker raised and about to strike; BESS screams]

EMERSON: No, please! I didn't mean it. Honest! I was just joking. Please. Ask them. I was just playing the game.

[Instantly changed, MULDOON lowers the poker calmly and returns it to its place]

MULDOON: Could never fool you, eh, Emerson?

[BESS gradually yields to giggles, SADIE is slightly amused, EMERSON recovers and rises]

EMERSON: Pretty good. No, really. I mean it. You had me going.
BESS: He got you back, didn't he?
EMERSON: Ah, I knew he was joking.

[MULDOON fixes drinks at the bar]

MULDOON: That's right. Never concede a thing.
BESS: Oh, come on, dear. He fooled you. Admit it.
EMERSON: I was just playing along.
SADIE: What some people will do for fun.
EMERSON: He's good though.
BESS: Well, he fooled me. I thought he was really…
EMERSON: Well, some of us were meant to be fooled more easily than others. We were just having a little joust. He's good though. I mean that. You do it well.
MULDOON: Thank you. Some of us were…

[A knock at the door]

Well, well, well, who could that be?
EMERSON: No way. Probably the neighbor about the noise.
SADIE: Don't bet on it, honey.

[MULDOON answers the door. FOSDICK steps in.]

MULDOON: What a surprise! To some of us in any case.
SADIE: Just in the neighborhood?
MULDOON: Do come in. Feel at home. Have a drink. [hands him one] Have two. [hands him another, shuts the door, returns and take a drink back] Well?
FOSDICK: I'm not through here.
MULDOON: Not through? What could you mean?
FOSDICK: I didn't concede.
MULDOON: You left. We all watched you leave. One could consider that a...
FOSDICK: I came back.
MULDOON: So you did. No doubt you've pondered the mysteries of the universe. You've reached into the deepest rut of your shallow perception and came up empty. Still, you came back. You came back because your instinct is stronger than your reason. Well?
FOSDICK: I'm not leaving until we've finished. I have not conceded and I won't. Not now, not ever. I'm telling you flat out: I will never concede.
MULDOON: [shrugs] We'll see. [FOSDICK sits] Do sit down.
FOSDICK: Thank you. I am sitting.
MULDOON: So you are.

[Long silence. During the following silences FOSDICK and EMERSON are baffled, groping for words. BESS is amused, giggling sporadically. SADIE is quiet, content, drinking. MULDOON is intently quiet.]

MULDOON: Could you serve the next round, Bess?
BESS: Sure. [crosses to bar] I know everyone but yours,

Mr. Fosdick.
>FOSDICK: Anything's fine with me.
>BESS: Anything it is. [giggles]

[Silence]

>BESS: [serving] Oh, Mr. Fosdick, you already have a drink.
>FOSDICK: So I do.
>MULDOON: So you do.

[Silence]

>EMERSON: Is somebody going to say something?
>FOSDICK: [momentarily] I can't stand silence.

[Silence]

>BESS: Nice weather we're having.
>FOSDICK: Yes, it is. Except for the rain.

END ACT ONE.

ACT TWO

(Lights up slowly. Everything is exactly as it was. Long silence.)

EMERSON: You know, it's a funny thing about that rain.
FOSDICK: It certainly is.
EMERSON: It just started out of nowhere.
FOSDICK: I noticed that.
EMERSON: I think it's the ozone layer. Like I was telling Bess...
BESS: I don't give a damn about the rain! [realizes she's broken character] Oh. [giggles]
FOSDICK: I'm not particularly concerned myself.
EMERSON: I was just...making...conversation.

[Silence. Lights fade to spot on SADIE.]

SADIE: Oh great! [to Muldoon] Now what am I supposed to do?
MULDOON: Improvise, my dear, improvise.
SADIE: Improvise? The man says improvise! Sure, Mac. The last time someone said that to me I was driving this little foreign job, right? I'm driving from here to...some resort or something...up in the mountains, you know? We wanted to get away from it all. So anyway, I'm going up this narrow mountain road, you know? The kind you can kill yourself on, looking at the scenery and all, and it starts getting dark. And I'm driving through this canyon with the beautiful scenery and the rocks and the cliffs and the five thousand foot drop, right? And it's getting dark. So no problem, I calmly reach over to turn the headlights on...and

the windshield wipers come on. So it's sloshing around with the little squirt every half turn and I'm staying cool. I'm not upset. I turn the radio on, the defrost, the electronic scanner, push in the lighter...twice. I mess around with the power windows for a while, smoke me a cigarette and then it hits me. I don't know how to operate this car. So I lean over to the sleeping beauty in the seat next to me, who happens to own the damn thing, and say: Hey sweetheart, it suddenly occurs to me that I don't know how to operate your car! He wakes up just enough to raise his right eye into a squint, you know? He smiles and says: Improvise.

[to Muldoon] I survived that one. I'll survive this one. If I'm anything at all, I'm a survivor. [sudden flash] Oh. I just remembered what I wanted to say. I don't really belong here. I just came to a party, you know? I always just come to a party. A friend says: You want to go to a party? I say: Sure, do we know them? Some of them turn out really strange. Like this one. But I survive. Sometimes I wonder if what I really want is...not to. At least this one's amply supplied in the booze department. Who am I to complain when there's free booze around? [spot fades] I guess that means it's over.

[SADIE crosses to the bar for another drink as the general lighting comes up. MULDOON is standing by the bookshelves reading. Long silence.]

EMERSON: Damn it! Somebody say something!
BESS: Oh! Well...let's see...

[Silence]

EMERSON: This could drive a sane man straight over a cliff!
FOSDICK: Maybe if you quit talking about it.
EMERSON: Quit talking? [laughs] That's the damned

problem! [silence] I wonder…if…damn it!

[Silence. Lights fade to spot on MULDOON.]

MULDOON: [reading] "And so I am reduced to this: That I can think of no meaning that justifies this passing. That I can no longer perceive the purpose of this existence. Is this not the fatal thought of the philosopher's final torment? Once, long, long ago, from a time when it promised sweet immortality, I theorized that a man dies when the meaning of his life fades into nonexistence. The promise now is one of doom – dark, dank, foreboding. The death knell sounds its tired drum and I sit listening, paralyzed and accepting. And if I live a thousand years or if tomorrow is the last day of my drudgery, this present state of mind christens my impending death."

[Spot out. Lights up. MULDOON has discarded his book. Silence.]

EMERSON: [glances at his watch] Gee wiz! Look at the time! Well, Bess, I think we'd better be getting home.
BESS: Yes, dear, it's about that time.
EMERSON: Sadie? Are you ready?
SADIE: That's my cue. Sure I'm ready…as soon as I finish this drink.
MULDOON: But you're ready now, aren't you? I'd be more than pleased to give Sadie a ride at her convenience.
EMERSON: Sadie?
MULDOON: I don't do this sort of thing often. It's not my nature. So please allow me this favor.
SADIE: It's fine with me. I'm just along for the ride.
EMERSON: Fine. [rises to exit, BESS follows] I'd like to thank you for a very interesting evening.
BESS: Yes, thank you.

MULDOON: You're too kind.

EMERSON: Not at all. I'll look forward to our next little get together.

MULDOON: Who knows?

EMERSON: Mr. Fosdick, I'll see you Sunday morning.

FOSDICK: Eight o'clock at the clubhouse.

EMERSON: Don't be late.

FOSDICK: I wouldn't think of it.

EMERSON: Fine, good. [to Muldoon] You'll see that the lady gets home safely?

MULDOON: You have my word.

EMERSON: Fine, good. Well then, goodnight.

BESS: Bye-bye everyone!

OTHERS: Goodnight, Bye Bess, etc.

[BESS and EMERSON exit]

FOSDICK: So what was that about?

MULDOON: Call it an amusement, an observation of human behavior under controlled conditions. I found it very educational. It gave me a chance to observe you with your peers, Fosdick. It provided an opportunity to confirm my beliefs.

FOSDICK: The results?

MULDOON: You're a very ugly man, Fosdick.

FOSDICK: That's comforting and predictable. What is your opinion of my peers?

MULDOON: Emerson? A shallow version of you. Bess? Something of a waste. She collects sympathy like some collect trinkets. She may be very intelligent, witty, creative... In fact, I believe she is a fascinating specimen beneath the mundane exterior she chooses to wear but, alas, we'll never know.

FOSDICK: What about Sadie? As a fellow member of the species, what is your opinion of Sadie?

MULDOON: It is impolite to speak in the presence of

another as if she does not exist.

SADIE: No, I'd like to hear it.

FOSDICK: She'd like to hear it.

MULDOON: Okay. Sadie is the surprise of the story. She really should have made her exit with the others.

FOSDICK: Why didn't she?

SADIE: It isn't polite to speak about someone as if she's not present.

FOSDICK: My apologies.

SADIE: Forget it. I have.

FOSDICK: But I haven't. Why are you still here? You hate game playing. Or is that just an act?

SADIE: I'm not playing games. I'm finishing a drink. After that who knows I might finish another.

FOSDICK: You don't think for a minute Muldoon would have you stay to finish a drink.

SADIE: Actually I thought it was for my charm and wit. I'm a charming and witty woman, you know.

MULDOON: Frustrating, isn't it, Fosdick. You're not used to confronting a woman who doesn't back down. You can't conceive a woman who can beat you at your own game though she isn't even playing.

FOSDICK: Truthfully, I find Sadie charming and witty. I'm intrigued.

SADIE: Thanks I'm sure. Maybe I'll crash at you place.

MULDOON: Indeed. Charming, witty and frustrating. Shall I call your bluff?

FOSDICK: I admit it. This time. Who's keeping score?

MULDOON: You can't stand anyone who refuses to play the game. It amuses me to watch you squirm like a worm in a puddle of fresh rain.

FOSDICK: First, she is playing. She's just cleverer than you and I. Second, this is your game, not mine. You can't pin it on me. Finally, I have not been defeated. I have not conceded. Where there is no concession, there is no victory.

MULDOON: Wrong in the first instance. Wrong in the second. Correct in the third. How did you come up with it?

FOSDICK: I have a good mentor. One of the best. A master of the game.

MULDOON: Do you?

FOSDICK: I believe so.

MULDOON: It's too late for banter, Fosdick. The evening is growing long. Let's drill down to the marrow, shall we? Sadie, feel free to refill your drink as it pleases you. Feel free to comment or not, to participate or observe.

SADIE: I do and will. [crosses to the bar] Thanks.

MULDOON: You're a guest in this house, Fosdick, yet we know nothing of you. You're like a stranger who snuck in the back way and remains among us. Isn't it time we found out who Fosdick is?

FOSDICK: I'm just like you, Muldoon, only before the fall.

MULDOON: Everything in its own time. We need background. We need facts. Are you married?

FOSDICK: Yes I am.

MULDOON: Happily?

FOSDICK: [hesitates] Yes.

MULDOON: I detect uncertainty. Yes or no?

FOSDICK: Yes. I suppose.

MULDOON: Children?

FOSDICK: A boy and a girl.

MULDOON: Do you often leave your family for fun and games with strangers?

FOSDICK: I do not.

MULDOON: You play golf?

FOSDICK: Yes.

MULDOON: Racquetball, tennis, poker, bowling, chess?

FOSDICK: Yes. I see your point. I don't, however, often leave my family for fun and games with strangers.

MULDOON: Tonight is an exception?

FOSDICK: It is.

MULDOON: It's an exceptional evening.

FOSDICK: I would say so.

MULDOON: Have you telephoned your wife?

FOSDICK: I'll be candid. She thinks I'm on a business trip.

MULDOON: A business trip?

FOSDICK: It was cancelled. I didn't want to worry her.

MULDOON: Bullshit, Fosdick. You didn't want to explain yourself to her. Tonight of all nights you are cheating on your wife!

FOSDICK: What should I have said? I'll be spending the evening in verbal combat with someone I've never met?

MULDOON: Yes. That's what you're doing, isn't it? That's what you enjoy doing. I can assure you your wife would only have been surprised by your candor.

FOSDICK: She would have been very surprised. This is an exceptional evening. I've never done anything like this.

MULDOON: Shall we ask Sadie what she thinks of deceitful husbands?

SADIE: Leave me out of it. Play with yourselves. Knock each other out. What do I care? I'll go it alone if you don't mind.

FOSDICK: I don't mind. Do you mind, Muldoon?

MULDOON: Not at all. Have you considered divorce?

FOSDICK: Frankly, Muldoon, I have.

MULDOON: *You* have – not *we* but you.

FOSDICK: I can only speak for myself.

MULDOON: But you've never gone through with it. Why?

FOSDICK: We've always been able to reconcile.

MULDOON: Not *you* but *we*. Curious, isn't it?

FOSDICK: We've argued. We've fought. What couple hasn't? We've had our problems, our differences, our little wars over God knows what but we've always been able to forgive and forget. So far.

MULDOON: You really are being candid.

FOSDICK: I suspect...I assume it will come to that in the end.

MULDOON: The final conflict? The battle to decide it all? How old are the children?

FOSDICK: Seven and nine.

MULDOON: Seven years. The wonders of birth control.

FOSDICK: She started taking the pill. Then she stopped.

MULDOON: Stopped taking the pill?

FOSDICK: That's right. It was no longer necessary.

MULDOON: No longer necessary?

FOSDICK: Please stop repeating. Surely a man as capable as you can overcome his natural tendencies.

MULDOON: I apologize. Frankly I'm stunned by your sudden frankness but I can't let this pass.

FOSDICK: I'd rather not be explicit. There's a lady in the house.

SADIE: Don't worry about me, honey. I've heard everything. Nothing shocks me anymore.

FOSDICK: We don't screw much anymore.

MULDOON: Much?

FOSDICK: Occasionally. Usually after a fight. I wear a condom.

MULDOON: Can't be much fun in that.

FOSDICK: There isn't as a matter of fact.

MULDOON: Did she use it as a weapon? The refusal of it, that is.

FOSDICK: Not very effectively.

MULDOON: I see. Do the children know of their poor father's trials and tribulations?

FOSDICK: They know infinitely more of their mother's. She spends half the day on the subject. The rest of the time they're either in school or asleep.

MULDOON: Thank God for public education.

FOSDICK: Thank God for sleep.

MULDOON: She uses them against you. And you?
FOSDICK: I'm hardly ever home.
MULDOON: Nevertheless, as the father figure you must have considerable influence even in your absence.
FOSDICK: I do manage to strike a few blows for fatherhood. She paints me as a monster. When I don't act the part, when I take them out for carnivals or treats or ball games, whatever, it enrages my wife.
MULDOON: Have you ever chippied on the lady?
FOSDICK: Have I what?
SADIE: [looks up] He really doesn't know. [rises, crosses to bar] I'll have that refill now.
MULDOON: Chippy? Cheat? Have you screwed another woman while you were married to your wife?
FOSDICK: [waits] I have.
MULDOON: You horned devil you.
FOSDICK: I'm not ashamed.
MULDOON: Things happen.
FOSDICK: It was a long time ago.
MULDOON: Was it?
FOSDICK: A very long time.
MULDOON: A little fun and games?
FOSDICK: A man has needs.
MULDOON: Were you seduced?
FOSDICK: I seduced her.
MULDOON: Seriously? I'm impressed.
FOSDICK: It was only a romantic interlude. It had no meaning and it served a purpose.
MULDOON: Did you tell your wife about it?
FOSDICK: I did. I took the fall. My wife is free to divorce me any time she likes. On her terms. We're up front about it now.
MULDOON: A conscientious adulterer, how quaint. Was it civil?
FOSDICK: The confrontation? Not exactly.

MULDOON: She got angry?
FOSDICK: She did. Very angry.
MULDOON: You got angrier.
FOSDICK: As a matter of fact...
MULDOON: Said you shouldn't have told her in the first place.
FOSDICK: That's exactly what I said.
MULDOON: Good move, Fosdick. Predictable but sound. And then what happened?
FOSDICK: That's the whole story.
MULDOON: Kissed and made up?
FOSDICK: [smiles] Not exactly.
MULDOON: Screwed and made up?
FOSDICK: That's right.

[They share a moment of bemusement, followed by silence.]

SADIE: What is this? The seventh inning stretch?
MULDOON: An accurate analogy. You better watch this man, Sadie. Turns out he's a sexual deviate.
SADIE: In that case, neither of us had better turn our backs.
FOSDICK: You've got nothing to worry about.
SADIE: Why's that? Not good enough for you?
MULDOON: Not enough tits and ass, eh Fosdick?
FOSDICK: Sadie's tits and ass are very much to my liking.
SADIE: What is it then? You don't like my style? A little too aggressive for your taste?
FOSDICK: [shaking his head] I don't make a play for another man's woman.
SADIE: You think we're a couple?
FOSDICK: It's obvious.
SADIE: I'm nobody's lady – nobody but my own.
FOSDICK: So you say.

SADIE: A selective deviate. I know the type.

MULDOON: Actually, he's a conscientious deviate. There is a difference.

SADIE: He rapes me and apologizes. Is that it?

MULDOON: Something like that.

FOSDICK: Bullshit, Muldoon! I'm calling bullshit!

SADIE: I think he's getting upset.

FOSDICK: I'm not but we're wasting time. Let's cut the crap and get down to it.

MULDOON: No more bullshit? Bullshit. We can't not bullshit. It's in the blood. It's a part of our wiring. We can't escape it. However, I stand corrected. You're not a deviate at all, Fosdick. Your perversion is in the mainstream.

FOSDICK: Fine. You stand corrected. Let's leave it at that and get on with it.

MULDOON: Let's talk about that job of yours, shall we?

FOSDICK: Not just yet. It's my turn.

MULDOON: Who's making the rules here? All of a sudden we're taking turns?

FOSDICK: Common courtesy. You had a go at my marriage, now it's my turn.

MULDOON: [considers] Fine. [silence] Is there a time limit?

FOSDICK: I'm sorry. I'm drawing a blank.

MULDOON: Pitiful, isn't he? Poor pitiful Fosdick can't summon a thought. Could it be there's nothing to think of?

FOSDICK: Give me a moment. I just can't think.

MULDOON: That is a problem. Maybe we can help or am I without flaws, without weakness, without faults?

FOSDICK: You're a vile, cruel and vicious man.

MULDOON: Aren't we all? Cruel and vicious that is. As for vile, my cynicism is harmless and of little concern to you.

FOSDICK: What is it that you live for? What is it that

you cherish? You contribute nothing to society. You have nothing. You're as empty as poor man's wallet.

MULDOON: I have this moment, this triumphant moment, this moment of truth. What else do I need? What else is there? This is my contribution, Fosdick: the stark, naked and unbearable truth!

FOSDICK: [considers] It's not a fair match.

MULDOON: Not fair?

FOSDICK: You have nothing to lose. You believe in nothing. Nothing can move you.

MULDOON: To the contrary, Fosdick, I'm moved right now.

FOSDICK: Bullshit! I'm calling your bluff!

MULDOON: Deeply, deeply moved.

FOSDICK: You're lying. [turns to Sadie] He's lying!

SADIE: Is he? You don't know the man.

FOSDICK: [considers] I don't believe it. He said it himself: there are no weaknesses. There's nothing I could possibly say that would knock him off his game.

SADIE: Nothing? The man is a weakness. He's a loser just like I am. A valiant, clever and highly intelligent loser. And what are you? A class one fool because you can't even see it.

MULDOON: [at the bookshelves reading] "He is one who knows not what he wants nor how to get what he thinks he wants; he cannot be even superficially happy." [closes book] A moment of truth brought to you by a moment of doubt, reflection and compassion.

FOSDICK: [to Sadie] What's he talking about?

SADIE: You really are hopeless. You can't even see it when it stands up and dances naked in front of you.

MULDOON: Dear, dear Sadie, hard lady, it takes one to know one.

SADIE: While we're trading clichés: Sad but true.

MULDOON: [considers] I'm wrong and I apologize. I'm a loser, not you. You've had it rough but you keep fighting back. You're a survivor. You've been abused, laughed at, kicked and subjected to God only knows what deviant actions men can throw at you, but you keep getting up and fighting back. I admire you, Sadie, more than you'll ever know. When I grow up I want to be just like you. And then there's Fosdick. Poor pitiful Fosdick with his rules and strategies and who keeps score. You're a fool, Fosdick, and the biggest loser of us all.

FOSDICK: No concession.

MULDOON: No victory. No victory, no defeat. True. You haven't lost...yet. But you're a loser just the same and you're losing tonight. Are you aware of that?

FOSDICK: [to Sadie] What was he saying? "He is one who knows...?"

SADIE: What do you think I am, an interpreter? I'm not playing, remember?

FOSDICK: I'm not asking you to play.

MULDOON: She's not playing. You want to know what I said? You want another pass? Ask me. You want to know what it means? Ask me. We'll make it a rule: Ask me and I'll tell you.

FOSDICK: Fine, what did you mean?

MULDOON: What did I mean when?

FOSDICK: Stop!

MULDOON: You have to follow along, Fosdick. To follow a conversation requires listening. If you don't listen we'll never make it through the night.

FOSDICK: Come on, quit jerking me around. Your moment of truth. Your pearl of wisdom. Your confession.

MULDOON: "He is one who knows not what he wants nor how to get what he thinks he wants; he cannot be even superficially happy."

FOSDICK: Yes, yes. What does it mean?

MULDOON: You want to know what it means? I'll tell you what it means. It's a rule after all: You ask and I tell you. It means I'm hanging by a thread. It's all I have left after all I've let go.

FOSDICK: I see.

MULDOON: Do you? No, you don't. I've told you but you don't see, you can't see, you're a blind man playing darts. Do you know what you're looking for, Fosdick? Do you know what it looks like, what it smells like, what it tastes and feels like? Do you even have a clue?

FOSDICK: It's a work in progress.

MULDOON: A thread, Fosdick. One thin thread and I go tumbling, feet over head, gasping for air like a fish out of water. I'm a stranger in a strange land reaching out for the end. Concession, victory, end of evening, sleep. But you've no idea, do you?

FOSDICK: I don't believe you.

MULDOON: Then call my bluff.

FOSDICK: It won't work. You don't follow the rules.

MULDOON: [considers] Then concede.

FOSDICK: Not a chance, Muldoon.

MULDOON: [pacing] Poor Fosdick. Poor pitiful ugly Fosdick. Watch his features change as his desperation grows. Watch his nose enlarge, his eyes redden and squint. Watch his cheeks droop into prominent jowls and a large hairy wart appear on his left eyelid. You think he's ugly now, just wait!

SADIE: Lay off, will ya?

MULDOON: You're ugly, Fosdick! And I'm going to make you see yourself before this night is over.

SADIE: You've gone far enough.

MULDOON: No, I haven't. I wish I had but I haven't.

SADIE: Why?

MULDOON: Why what?

SADIE: Tell me. I'd like to know. I've sat here, drinking my drinks, minding my own damned business, listening to this incredible overmatch. It's the 1927 Yankees against the little league all stars! Why? I keep telling myself: he wants me to be here. He wants me to witness this. Why? He wouldn't systematically destroy a helpless human being for fun and games, would he? Would you? [no response] Then, damn it, why?

MULDOON: [absorbs] Because every fool must be made to see what motivates him. And because...

SADIE: Because?

MULDOON: I can't say.

SADIE: Then I can't stay. [waits, rises] I'll get a cab.

MULDOON: I'll call you one.

SADIE: No, thanks. I'd like to walk. I'll be fine.

MULDOON: Sadie? [waits, deeply] I'm sorry.

SADIE: Oddly enough, I believe you. [to Fosdick, shaking hands] You're staying?

FOSDICK: For a while.

SADIE: [shrugs] See ya.

[Exit SADIE]

FOSDICK: [waits] You got rid of her.

MULDOON: I got rid of her? How did I manage that?

FOSDICK: Who knows? Maybe she's your whore. Maybe you have an understanding. I don't know the details but you got rid of her and I know why.

MULDOON: This should be interesting.

FOSDICK: Because she would have led me to that thread of yours.

MULDOON: Incredible.

FOSDICK: As sure as I'm standing here.

MULDOON: The way your mind works is beyond human understanding. What if I told you she already gave you all the answers you need?

FOSDICK: Save it, Muldoon. It won't work.

MULDOON: What precisely won't work?

FOSDICK: It's just you and me now. The smokescreen

won't work.

MULDOON: Call my bluff.

FOSDICK: We've covered that. It doesn't work if I don't believe you and I don't believe you.

MULDOON: That's enough of that. Rules are rules. This is my game. It is played by my rules and they are honored or there is no game.

FOSDICK: [considers] Okay. Fine. I believe you.

MULDOON: You believe me now.

FOSDICK: Yes.

MULDOON: Only a moment ago you accused me of being a liar and a cheat. How can you possibly believe a liar and a cheat?

FOSDICK: That's not what I said.

MULDOON: You implied.

FOSDICK: Yes.

MULDOON: Then you were lying.

FOSDICK: No. I believed it then.

MULDOON: You were crossing me.

FOSDICK: Yes. No. I don't know.

MULDOON: Yes. You were crossing me because you enjoy crossing me. Care to argue the point?

FOSDICK: Yes. I suggested you were cheating because I suspected it was true. I wanted to know if you were changing the rules or if there were any rules. I was just being honest.

MULDOON: Bullshit, Fosdick. You may have believed it was true but you were not being honest. You haven't been honest since you walked in the door with some half-witted dog story. You're not being honest now.

FOSDICK: It's only a game, Muldoon. Watch out. You're beginning to sound desperate. You're beginning to act like a loser.

MULDOON: Motive, Fosdick. Why are you here? Moment to moment, click by click, what moves you forward? What goads you on? Your last comment: The nearest stone within your grasp. Pick it up and give it a hurl. Why not?

FOSDICK: It's a natural reaction.

MULDOON: My point exactly. Now think about this entire evening. You came here for the express purpose of confrontation: Yes on no?

FOSDICK: Actually, no. I came here because I was concerned...

MULDOON: Bullshit, Fosdick. Will it never end? You came for a fight and stayed on the promise of war: Yes or no?

FOSDICK: No. It's only a game. Don't flatter yourself. You're not the world. You're not even a part of the world. This is just a game, a trivial and meaningless game.

MULDOON: You don't believe that.

FOSDICK: What's to believe? It's true.

MULDOON: This is a new tactic, isn't it?

FOSDICK: Call it whatever you want. I'm speaking about the truth and the truth is this entire evening has been nothing more and nothing less than a vulgar, twisted, deranged game. Cruel, vicious and ugly. This is your game, Muldoon. What do you think that says about you?

MULDOON: About me? I live here. This is my life. I can't escape it. But you! You volunteered for it. You went out of your way to find it, left and came back for more! And you're still here! I can't get rid of you!

FOSDICK: Sure you can. It only requires two little words.

MULDOON: Incredible. Your life has been reduced to a meaningless, trifling and inept charade, yet you're still concerned with winning and losing.

FOSDICK: Don't flatter yourself, Muldoon. My life is as it always has been, as it was yesterday, as it will be tomorrow. Nothing in my life has changed.

MULDOON: [considers] True. Incredibly, indelibly and

tragically true.

FOSDICK: There is no tragedy. Tragedy is for distorted minds, Muldoon, like yours. If it seems ugly to you take a good look in the mirror. This is your game.

MULDOON: You are as you always were. Nothing I could do or say could change that. Certainly not my game. [waits] What? Running out of string? Chased it as far as your feeble intellect can go without bumping up against a wall? Empty? Lost? Can the fool see what motivates him?

FOSDICK: I've followed your lead. Nothing more, nothing less. You are my mentor. Remember?

MULDOON: You are as you always were. Your own words. Only now you stand naked. You have nothing and no one to hide behind. You're exposed.

FOSDICK: Exposed? To what? Have I done something to offend you? What crimes have I committed? What horrible things have I done? Go ahead, Muldoon, expose me.

MULDOON: It isn't what you've done but why. You have used everything at your disposal to thwart me. You have branded me a liar and a cheat because, frankly, you could think of nothing else. You've kicked and scratched like a cornered beast. You've groped for clues and begged for answers, whimpering like a frightened puppy on a leash. Why, Fosdick, why?

FOSDICK: It's what you do and not what you think that matters.

MULDOON: It's what you think that moves you.

FOSDICK: It's just a game.

MULDOON: Think, Fosdick. Think about your life: battle after battle in a disgusting march through existence. Think about your wife and why you married in the first place.

FOSDICK: You're wrong about that. We married for love.

MULDOON: I'm impressed. That you could have the mendacity to even utter that word in the context of your marriage. Tell me about it.

FOSDICK: [sighs] We met in high school. Later, years later, we dated. We found we had common interests. We fell in love. I asked her to marry me. We were happy in the beginning. Enchanted. We loved each other very much.

MULDOON: Before the fall? I don't doubt that you loved her, Fosdick, but you craved an opponent far more than love. So did she. Why else would she marry you? That is why you married and why you remain married when all the love has flittered away like the last butterfly of spring.

FOSDICK: Was it any different for you?

MULDOON: [considers] I never married and I've never used a child as battering ram for my wars. I've never used a child as a toy to be bounced around in my vicious games.

FOSDICK: That's not fair. I support my family. I'm a responsible father and my children can depend on me.

MULDOON: You'd leave them.

FOSDICK: I would not.

MULDOON: Ever consider divorce? Motive, Fosdick, motivation. You will divorce because that battle is more important to you than all the love, the family and the children. The battle to climax a series of battles and you'll enjoy every minute of it. And then, even before it ends, you will have found new battles to fight, new campaigns to plot and new wars to wage. Why are you here?

FOSDICK: I believe in my family. I love my children. I love my wife even now. If it ends in divorce I'll still be a good father. Love, Muldoon, love is my motive.

MULDOON: Please, Fosdick, that you could even say that is pitiful. That you could believe it is absurd.

FOSDICK: But I do believe it. That's what you'll never understand. Faith requires no reason.

MULDOON: You're a clown, Fosdick. A ridiculous clown with oversized shoes and a big red nose. I despise and pity you.

FOSDICK: You pity me? That's a laugh. Pity the poor

boy who has nothing to live for. What a joke! You're the one who needs pity.

MULDOON: Need? I don't even believe in it.

FOSDICK: That's right. You believe in nothing.

MULDOON: And you believe in nothing but conflict. The glow of battle, the thrill of victory, the taste of blood on your vile, pitiful lips.

FOSDICK: I believe in love. That's right. I believe in family. I believe in a society of equal opportunity. I believe in law and order. And yes, I believe in God.

MULDOON: No, Fosdick, that won't do.

FOSDICK: A man's faith is his temple. It's sacred. You can no more question a man's faith than you can the existence of the soul.

MULDOON: Nothing is sacred and everything can and must be challenged by reason – including the very concept of God, a nebulous and vague construct that has a thousand different meanings to a thousand people.

FOSDICK: That's what God is: Magnanimous. Omnipresent. It's everything to everyone. That's why God is God.

MULDOON: God. The catch-all be-all answer to the mystery of the universe, a mystery that contains an infinite variety of mysteries, each with a myriad of questions. Someone whom no one can recall answered: God! Infinity to one, Fosdick. Take your chances. I won't condemn you for it but don't expect me to be bowled over by the invocation of God.

FOSDICK: Faith, Muldoon, you can't escape it. I'm a Christian. I go to church regularly and faithfully. I have since childhood. I offer that not to win you to the cause but as proof of my sincerity.

MULDOON: It only proves what I already know: that you'll do anything to defeat your opponent. What is the church but a leach on society? It is a place to plot battles, conspire against your fellows, consolidate wealth, exploited for any number of reasons: moral, immoral, corrupt or incorruptible. It makes no difference. But it is nothing of itself. No, Fosdick. Try again. We need something we can put our hands on. Something you at least have some reasonable conception of.

FOSDICK: [shrugs] My religion, my values, my family, my wife. My God, what else is there?

MULDOON: Think, Fosdick, think. What is it that you live for? What's the first thing that enters your brain when you wake up in the morning? What makes you a living, breathing, dynamic being instead of a token in some mindless and vicious game?

FOSDICK: [considers] My job. Of course. That must be the answer.

MULDOON: Somehow I knew it would come down to this.

FOSDICK: It had to, didn't it? A man is what a man does. A man's job is a measure of his social worth. If he does his job well he is a valued member of his tribe.

MULDOON: Do you? Do your job well?

FOSDICK: Very well.

MULDOON: Any promotions lately?

FOSDICK: I've climbed the corporate ladder slowly but surely.

MULDOON: Who'd you have to step on in the process?

FOSDICK: It's not up to me who gets left behind. That's just how it works.

MULDOON: Is it?

FOSDICK: Of course. I like my job. I'm industrious, diligent, always willing to go the extra mile. I've got the experience and the evaluations to back me up.

MULDOON: Of course: Industrious, enthusiastic, a very promising prospect. Translation: He's beginning to show the talons of cold-hearted greed. Thrives on a good fight. Good soldier to have at your side. No stakes too high.

JACK RANDOM

Poor old Harry: He was a good man in his day but he became a burden... Sound familiar, Fosdick?

FOSDICK: How the hell did you know?

MULDOON: I didn't. How could I?

FOSDICK: I suppose not.

MULDOON: No denial?

FOSDICK: No denial. But no concession either.

MULDOON: That's right. Hold out to the end. If you're caught in the act, deny it. Never give in. Think again, Fosdick.

FOSDICK: Why? I'm tired thinking. We both know it's a futile process. I can't possibly give you what you want and you refuse to give me what I want. We're just jacking off here.

MULDOON: You're giving up? You're quitting? Don't play the fool, Fosdick. Can't you see? One small, petty example to give your life meaning – or at least a glimpse of meaning – and I concede.

FOSDICK: I can't do it. I'm tired. It's late.

MULDOON: You can. You must. Think, Fosdick.

FOSDICK: It's no use.

MULDOON: Try. Search your past for one brief moment of compassion, of genuine humanity. For God's sake, Fosdick, to save *my* soul....

FOSDICK: [waits] To save *your* soul?

MULDOON: [waits] Yes. To save my soul and yours.

FOSDICK: [waits] I'm sorry. It's pointless. There's nothing there.

MULDOON: There is. There must be. Somewhere, sometime you must have been human. You weren't born this way.

FOSDICK: Wasn't I? A thread, Muldoon. A needle in the proverbial haystack. We don't even know what we're looking for. Do we?

MULDOON: Hope, Fosdick. In a word: hope. Search. Search the deepest place in your heart. When you leave here, where will you turn for consolation? What gives you hope?

FOSDICK: [waits] I can only think of one possibility.

MULDOON: [waits] What is it?

FOSDICK: Now look, Muldoon, this is it. It's your last chance. If you reject it outright, that's it. It's over. There is no other answer.

MULDOON: What is it?

FOSDICK: Patience, Muldoon. The question is: What is there when all else fails? Who do I turn to when there is no one left? The answer...the only possible answer...is the family.

MULDOON: [acutely disappointed] No.

FOSDICK: Accept it! There's nothing else.

MULDOON: No, damn you, no!

FOSDICK: Love is hope, is it not?

MULDOON: There is no more love. Love cannot survive in a world where mendacity, greed and bigotry thrive. We turned our backs on love. You had it for a while, a very short while, and you discarded it like an old rusted tool that has no more use. Love is dead, Fosdick. Murdered. And the executioner was promoted.

FOSDICK: [shakes head] That's it then. It's all over.

MULDOON: It's not over. It's never over.

FOSDICK: It is for me.

MULDOON: [sudden anger] Do you think I'm some kind of god? If I accept it then it's so? How can I believe what you don't believe yourself? Out of pity or desperation? There is no more pity. There is only the truth and the desperate hour is upon us.

FOSDICK: I can't help you, Muldoon. My time is up. I've had it with this game of yours. I don't know where it leads or what purpose it serves but I do know this: Whatever it is, it isn't worth it.

MULDOON: Fosdick, I swear to you that I would push no man as I've pushed you for a game. I would expose no fellow being as I have you for an evening's pleasure. There is no pleasure and there is no game. Not at this point.

FOSDICK: What point is that?

MULDOON: The point from which there is no return. We've seen too much. We've learned too much. We know too much about our pathetic, miserable lives to turn back now.

FOSDICK: You've learned too much. You've seen too much. I've seen nothing but a vile, cruel, insane mind struggling, baiting, badgering and hating for no apparent reason.

MULDOON: You've seen a reflection of yourself and I have seen the same. You must see it.

FOSDICK: See what?

MULDOON: The truth. Reality. Yourself as you really are. Your life as it has been.

FOSDICK: I see nothing new – nothing that I haven't seen before.

MULDOON: [waits] Then you're right. It's over. You can go now. It was all a mistake. You don't belong here. Go and leave me in peace.

FOSDICK: One more thing.

MULDOON: What's that.

FOSDICK: You slipped. You gave it away. "To save *your* soul." You wanted me to give you something to believe in but I couldn't do it. No one could. Because your warped mind couldn't accept anything that I value. That's why you're the loser and always will be.

MULDOON: You think you've nailed it, don't you? You think we're playing out the last hand and you're sitting on a full boat.

FOSDICK: Not really. I think I've negotiated a stalemate by default.

MULDOON: That's charitable. But tell me the truth, Fosdick: You've backed me into a corner by the sheer strength of your superior will. Isn't that it?

FOSDICK: I'm flattered, Muldoon. I appreciate it.

MULDOON: You could never outplay me or outsmart me or outmaneuver me…but you can outlast me.

FOSDICK: Exactly.

MULDOON: "He is one who knows not what he wants nor how to get what he thinks he wants; he cannot be even superficially happy."

FOSDICK: It's your epitaph, isn't it?

MULDOON: Congratulations, my good man. That's it precisely. Confirmed and sealed.

FOSDICK: Is that a concession?

MULDOON: [waits] I suppose it is. You win, Fosdick. [FOSDICK shakes hands and starts to leave] Just one more thing.

FOSDICK: You're kidding. What is it?

MULDOON: I have nothing. I admit it. No faith, no dreams, no ambitions and no hope. What gives you any more than I have?

FOSDICK: The game, Muldoon. I have the game.

MULDOON: The game is nothing.

FOSDICK: But I believe it is. That's enough for me.

[Exit FOSDICK. MULDOON stares after him, crosses to his desk, opens a manuscript, opens a drawer, pulls out a pistol and places it on the desk. He scribbles a few lines in the manuscript. A knock at the door. He looks up, replaces the gun and answers the door. It is SADIE who enters.]

SADIE: You didn't think I'd let you be alone tonight, did you?

MULDOON: One never knows.

[They embrace. Lights out.]

END ACT TWO.

NIGHTHAWKS CAFE

(The Boulevard of Broken Dreams)

SETTING

A diner in the forgotten part of a large city. Gottfried Helnwein's adaptation of Edward Hopper's *Nighthawks*. It is a typical diner with a long, curving counter with fixed, rotating stools and tables lining rows of windows dividing the diner from the outside world.

It is the evening of a welcoming party. As the curtain opens John is expected later in the evening.

CHARACTERS

BOGIE: Humphrey Bogart with fedora as he appeared in *Casa Blanca*.

COUNTRY: Elvis Presley in his pre-Vegas days.

DEAN: James Dean with leather jacket as he appeared in *East of Eden*.

BLONDIE: An elegant Marilyn Monroe as she appeared in *Gentlemen Prefer Blondes*.

JOHN: John Lennon as he appeared on the cover of *Sergeant Pepper's Lonely Hearts Club Band*.

ACT ONE

(COUNTRY is behind the counter, wearing an apron and tending to his business, cleaning up and wiping down. BOGIE sits on an upstage stool staring into his cup of coffee. He finishes it off.)

BOGIE: Hey Country, shoot me again straight up.
COUNTRY: Sure Boge.

[COUNTRY pulls a pint bottle from behind the counter and spices Bogie's coffee with gin.]

BOGIE: Where is everyone?
COUNTRY: Last minute errands I suppose.
BOGIE: Last minute? For what?
COUNTRY: The party.
BOGIE: We're having a party? Who's it for?
COUNTRY: New kid in town. They call him Johnny.
BOGIE: Johnny?
COUNTRY: Yep.
BOGIE: Must be a big deal. What's he do?
COUNTRY: Nothing, Boge. He's coming here.
BOGIE: Don't play the wise guy. You're no good at it. What did he do before he was coming here – downstairs when it counted.
COUNTRY: He was a singer.
BOGIE: I see. Another singer. Like you used to be.
COUNTRY: Yep.
BOGIE: I'm guessing he's not your style from your less than enthusiastic reaction.
COUNTRY: Mister, nobody's got my style.
BOGIE: That's not the way I hear it. I hear there were

several thousand who had your style down to the last detail. The way you combed your hair, the way you moved your hips, the way you spoke in broken sentences, even the way you sang. Hell, if you were to go back down there today they wouldn't even recognize you. There's too many just like you. As it is up here, we don't even know if you're the real deal. Might be an imposter for all we know.

COUNTRY: [smiles] Don't you believe it, Boge. They said the same about you.

BOGIE: That's right, kid. For all you know I'm the imposter.

COUNTRY: I know the genuine article when I see it.

BOGIE: Thanks kid. So do I. No matter how meticulous the imitation, a copy is still just a copy. It can never capture the essence. That's why they still talk about us, kid. That's why they'll go on talking about us for a hundred years. Just the same, a man can't be too careful. Did he write his own songs?

COUNTRY: That's what they tell me. Had a partner he wrote with.

BOGIE: Yeah? You didn't do a lot of writing, did ya, Country?

COUNTRY: Didn't have to. Had more writers than a poor dog has fleas. I did some writing. Never got around to singing most of them.

BOGIE: Well, looks like you'll be staying behind the counter.

COUNTRY: I don't mind. I may have grabbed that old ring of fame and fortune but I'm just a country boy at heart. Ain't afraid of working for a living.

BOGIE: Well, my friend, that's why you're there.

COUNTRY: That's what they tell me.

BOGIE: Don't you believe it, kid. Not that it's any of my business but you ought to get off your ass and sing a few songs once in a while. Bring a little life to this joint.

COUNTRY: This joint's got plenty of life without my

singing. Besides, you boys don't appreciate my kind of music. Cain't sing 'em just for my own amusement. It ain't in me.

BOGIE: We like them all right. Of course, we wouldn't mind a little blues once in a while. That gospel music you love so much is okay. It just seems like something's missing.

COUNTRY: Needs some backup singers.

BOGIE: Blondie's not good enough for you?

COUNTRY: She's all right. It's just that my kind of gospel needs some male voices. If I had my boys...

BOGIE: Yeah? Well, maybe that's it. That reminds me: When's Sam checking in? I've been expecting him.

COUNTRY: Didn't you hear? Sam checked in at a place the other end of town. Not his fault. He wanted to come here. Hear tell he asked about you. Sorry, Boge, I thought you knew.

BOGIE: No one tells me anything around here.

COUNTRY: Maybe we should go see him.

BOGIE: Yeah. We should go slumming one of these nights. Get out and see what the real people are like. Not tonight though. We've got a party.

COUNTRY: Tomorrow then. Do us good to get out of this joint for a while. Hang up a sign that says: Closed for the Evening.

BOGIE: Sure, sure. Maybe tomorrow.

COUNTRY: A man gets crazy staying in the same joint all the time.

BOGIE: You're right there.

COUNTRY: Do us some good.

BOGIE: I said all right, didn't I?

COUNTRY: [hesitates] You always say that, Boge, but you don't act on it. You stay in here night after night and talk about the good old days. It ain't right.

BOGIE: Who's telling who what's right and what ain't right? Besides, what else is there to talk about? The old days are all we have now.

COUNTRY: [waits] I guess you're right.

BOGIE: You're agreeing with me?

COUNTRY: You're the boss.

BOGIE: There ain't no boss here, kid. I wish there were. I'd stick it in his face.

COUNTRY: Whatever you say, Boge.

BOGIE: That's right. Whatever I say. [reflects] You're a fine one to be stuck with till the end of time. Can't you stand up for yourself once in a while?

COUNTRY: Like you did, Boge?

BOGIE: Yeah, like I did. There wasn't a man or woman on the planet who could tell me what to do and get away with it. [reflects] Well, maybe one.

COUNTRY: That director fellow? What's his name?

BOGIE: Huston? John Huston. Hell of a man. A man's man. Tough as nails. Wouldn't take crap from no one no how. Not the studio brass and certainly not the high paid prima donnas who call themselves actors! I told him more than once he should play Hemmingway! He was born for the role. [waits] No kid, that was in the movies. I wasn't talking about the movies. I was talking about real life.

COUNTRY: Who was it then?

BOGIE: [reflects] She was just a pup. Cute as a button. Smart mouthed, brash... I'll tell you what, kid, that little lady packed a wallop! Like Henry Armstrong against a club fighter, she'd come out swinging and deck you before you had time to tie your laces. Of course she could take it as well as she dished it out. Most of the time she was right. Hell, all of the time. She stuck up for herself and her own. That's what I admired about her. That's why she was my gal. She saved my life, kid.

[Silence. COUNTRY busies himself.]

BOGIE: What's with the silent treatment, kid?

RANDOM PLAYS

COUNTRY: Sorry. I know she was special.
BOGIE: Remind you of someone?
COUNTRY: Yeah, Boge, I guess she does.
BOGIE: Yeah? What's her name?
COUNTRY: Priscilla.
BOGIE: She was a young one too, wasn't she?
COUNTRY: She never turned on me no matter what went down.
BOGIE: Never turned on you? What would you call it?
COUNTRY: I let her down, Boge.
BOGIE: Stop being so hard on yourself, kid. A man does what a man's got to do. So you popped a few pills, took on a few pounds. A woman's supposed to stand by her man when the times get tough. She's supposed to be loyal.
COUNTRY: A dog is supposed to be loyal, Boge. A woman's supposed to be true.
BOGIE: All right. Was she? [no response] I see. You don't have anything to say. You will though. Eternity is a long time. A man's got to talk about things. Get things settled in his mind so he can sleep at night.
COUNTRY: My mind is settled. Just don't like to talk about it.
BOGIE: You will though. Maybe not today, maybe not tomorrow...but you will talk about it. It'll make you feel better. Mark my words. I used to hold things in with the best of them. It was eating me up inside. I was a tough guy. I could take a punch. Then I started talking and I've never stopped.
COUNTRY: [under his breath] You can say that again.
BOGIE: What's that?
COUNTRY: Nothing, Boge, just talking to myself.
BOGIE: That's not so. You were talking to me.
COUNTRY: Don't mean nothing by it. Just sort of slipped out.
BOGIE: What's got into you today? I sense a little

antagonism.

COUNTRY: Don't worry about it. It's nothing.

BOGIE: It's not nothing. It's something. I like a man who speaks his mind. Shows what he's worth. Keep it up, kid. We might get you out from behind the counter yet.

COUNTRY: Thanks, Boge, but I don't think so. Like I said, I don't mind.

BOGIE: Suit yourself. Too bad about Sam though. He'd have made a good addition to this place. Where'd he end up?

COUNTRY: Blue Bird, I think it was.

BOGIE: Blue Parrot?

COUNTRY: That's right.

BOGIE: Well whadya know? Funny he hasn't stopped by yet. We had some good times, Sam and I. During that shoot in Africa, the three of us were inseparable. We went everywhere together.

COUNTRY: Hear tell they keep him pretty busy.

BOGIE: Yeah? He always did like to keep busy. Says it keeps his mind off his troubles. So when's this party taking place?

COUNTRY: Who knows? When the time is right.

BOGIE: Yeah. Funny thing about Sam.

COUNTRY: Now don't you start.

BOGIE: Start what?

COUNTRY: You know what I'm talking about.

BOGIE: The beginning of a beautiful relationship? The end of what might have been?

COUNTRY: They'll be back soon. Any minute now.

BOGIE: So a man can't talk about the loves of his life? What can he talk about? I'm telling you, kid, this was the real thing. That woman had guts. More guts than any man I ever knew. They smeared her in the newspapers. Kicked her out of the movie business. Why? Because she had the guts to leave a man she didn't love and go with the one she did. It should have been me. At the time I didn't know. I was too worked up over contracts and career moves. There's some things a man can't get over. It gnaws at him. It picks him apart piece by piece until he finally faces up. Well, I faced it. But it's something I'll always think about. What might have been. I was lucky. Usually a man only gets one shot. If he misses it he'll be peddling newspapers the rest of his life. Me? I was the lucky one. I got another chance and I grabbed it. I grabbed it and held on for all it was worth. I didn't care what they said. So what if she was young? Who cares what they say in the newspapers? Not me, kid. I can thank Ingrid for that. I learned a hell of a lot from her and I don't care who knows it.

COUNTRY: Like another drink?

BOGIE: Sure, why not?

COUNTRY: I hear they've got a new singer over at the Bon Ami.

BOGIE: You wouldn't be trying to change the subject, would you?

COUNTRY: Maybe.

BOGIE: Why is that?

COUNTRY: I just don't like to see a lady cry, that's all.

BOGIE: Blondie?

COUNTRY: Yep.

BOGIE: Maybe she likes crying. Did that ever occur to you? Maybe what she's needs is a good cry. Shake something up inside. Let her hair down.

COUNTRY: The lady likes you, Bogie. She likes you a lot.

BOGIE: I like her too, kid. The whole world is enchanted by her. But let's not get carried away. Let's not forget where we are. It's like the movies, kid. It's not real.

COUNTRY: Seems real enough to me.

BOGIE: It may seem real but it's not. Let me ask you something, kid. Let's say we jump in the old Ford and drive down the boulevard to Main. Then we take a left and go down Magnolia. Then we drive out Kingston a couple miles.

COUNTRY: A couple miles?

BOGIE: Yes. A couple miles. Where would that take us?

COUNTRY: Cain't go that far.

BOGIE: I know we can't. That's the point. Where would we be?

COUNTRY: Nowheres.

BOGIE: Exactly. Nowhere. That's where we are now but we just don't know it. It seems like somewhere. There's something familiar about it. It's like someplace we used to know. But it's not real. It's a charade. Everything we say, everything we do and everything we feel we only seem to say, do and feel. It's as empty as an ingénue's lines. There's nothing behind it. It's a movie set.

COUNTRY: Maybe you're right. But she's a nice lady and I don't like to see her feelings hurt.

BOGIE: Just an old softy, aren't you?

COUNTRY: Guess so.

BOGIE: Just an old country boy seeing to it that everyone's fat and happy.

COUNTRY: What's wrong with that?

BOGIE: I'll tell you what's wrong with that. The truth. The truth isn't always nice. The truth doesn't always make people happy. But it's stubborn as hell and it has to be dealt with sooner or later.

COUNTRY: How about we deal with it later?

BOGIE: All right. I'll lay off for now if it'll make you feel better.

COUNTRY: Thanks Boge. I appreciate it.

[Enter DEAN and BLONDIE laughing. They carry shopping bags filled with memorabilia and party items. Dean settles at the counter. Blondie crosses around Bogie's back side and plants a kiss on his cheek.]

RANDOM PLAYS

BLONDIE: How's my leading man?

BOGIE: I'll bet you say that to all the bums on the boulevard.

BLONDIE: No. Just the one I adore.

BOGIE: How about it, Dean? Is that true?

DEAN: She only deals with marquee players.

BOGIE: Stop mumbling, kid. You're making me work too hard. How you got to be a star mumbling and whining through three motion pictures is something I'll never understand.

DEAN: [mumbling] There's a whole lot you'll never understand.

BOGIE: What's that, kid?

DEAN: [loud] Saw a film of yours the other day, the one where you play Pancho Villa. Nice work. Real deep.

BOGIE: I had a contract. I told you about that.

DEAN: I must have forgot.

BLONDIE: [rummaging through her bag] We got some simply wonderful things for the party. [pulls out the album cover of *Sergeant Peppers' Lonely Hearts Club Band*] Look at this! This is John! Isn't he cute? [indicates on the album cover] This is you, Country! And this is Dean, sullen and brooding. And here you are, Bogie! My, aren't you the saddest one! And here I am. Isn't it divine?

BOGIE: [taking the album] So this is John and his band. Sergeant Peppers.

COUNTRY: That's the album, Boge. His band was called *The Beatles*.

BOGIE: Did you know these guys?

COUNTRY: Sure. They all came down to Graceland to see me. Pay their respects to the King.

DEAN: All hail! The King is dead! Long live the King!

COUNTRY: It was a bit strange. Like I was old news or something. Like these boys was taking my place. They called it the British invasion.

JACK RANDOM

BOGIE: He's a Brit?

BLONDIE: They all were. John, Paul, George and Ringo. I think they're sweet and I just love their music! Would you like to hear it?

BOGIE: Save it, sweetheart. There's plenty of time for that. Remember Country's party? We don't want to get carried away. Country hasn't sung since.

COUNTRY: Y'all just don't like my kind of music.

BLONDIE: We love your music! [to Bogie, singing] Love me tender, love me true, never let me go, for it's here that I belong and I love you so. Love me tender, love me true, all my dreams fulfilled. For my darling, I love you and I always will.

COUNTRY: Thanks, sunshine. Some folks don't feel the same way you do.

BOGIE: Don't take it personally, kid. There's only so many times you can take a thing no matter how good it is. It's the same for all of us: Bus Stop, Niagara, East of Eden, Rebel without a Cause, the Maltese Falcon, hell, even Casa Blanca wears itself out in time. Isn't that right, Dean?

DEAN: That's right, Boge.

BOGIE: It doesn't mean we don't appreciate it. We do. But it's done. Now we're here and we've got to be concerned with who we are and who we were and why we did what we did. Not in the movies or the recording studio but in real life. That's why we're here and that's what we should be thinking about.

DEAN: Yeah, yeah, yeah.

BOGIE: What's on your mind, kid?

DEAN: The hell you say!

BOGIE: What's that suppose to mean?

DEAN: What does it mean? I'll tell you what it means, tough guy. You don't know why we're here any more than we do. That's what it means.

BOGIE: Well, well, well, the angry young man finally speaks in something more than a grunt or a whimper. I'm proud of you. I mean that. If you've got an idea, I'm listening.

DEAN: I just get tired of hearing the same thing over and over again. Jesus, Boge, don't you ever get tired of hearing yourself talk?

BOGIE: Yeah, I get tired of it. But somebody's got to do the talking. Somebody's got to do something. Otherwise we're just sitting around waiting for the next party.

BLONDIE: Don't take him seriously, Boge. We all get edgy when there's a party. It reminds us that time is still passing. And here we are. Nothing changes. It's enough to drive a girl mad. If it wasn't for you guys I don't know what I'd do.

COUNTRY: That goes for me too, Blondie.

BOGIE: Always trying to smooth things over, aren't you, Country? Always the peacemaker.

COUNTRY: I just don't understand why we've got to beat ourselves over the head is all. It's up to us to make the best of things the way they are.

BLONDIE: I'm all for that.

DEAN: She's right, Boge. I'm just feeling a little tense. I don't know what it is.

BOGIE: It's all right, kid. I'm not one to hold a grudge. Any time you've got something to say, come right out with it. I'll listen. I may not like it but I'll listen.

BLONDIE: Say Country, how about a little something to spice things up?

COUNTRY: I could never say no to a pretty lady. But go easy on it. It's early yet.

[COUNTRY pours her a drink.]

BLONDIE: I know it is. But I feel like I need a little extra today.

DEAN: Hit me one, Country. I'm feeling kind of wound

up myself.

COUNTRY: All around?

BOGIE: Deal me in. We all feel a little something today. I can't put my finger on it but there's something different about this one. It's got an edge to it.

BLONDIE: Whadya say we just relax and enjoy it? Take a load off. Let down our guards. How about it, Bogie?

BOGIE: Sure. I'm not one to spoil a party.

DEAN: [mumbles] Since when?

BOGIE: What's that, kid?

DEAN: Nothing. It's just...nothing.

BOGIE: There you go mumbling again. One of these days I'm going to grab you by your ears and shake you silly just to find out if there's anything in there.

DEAN: [mumbles] One of these days...

BOGIE: What's that, kid?

DEAN: [waits] One of these days we'll find out if you're man enough.

BOGIE: An interesting thought. How about today? How about right now?

COUNTRY: Say boys, I think you're forgetting something.

BOGIE: What's that, Country?

COUNTRY: There's a lady present.

BOGIE: Blondie doesn't mind. Do you, Blondie?

BLONDIE: No, I don't mind.

BOGIE: There, you see? The point is we'll never get anywhere with you always trying to smooth things over. Let's have it out. Put it all on the table and see where we stand.

DEAN: All right, Boge. You want to know what's eating me? I'll tell you what's eating me. All my life I've had people telling me what to do, what to think, what to say, what to feel, what not to feel. Women, agents, directors, friends, lovers, gurus and now you. You're not my father. You don't know the answers.

RANDOM PLAYS

BOGIE: That's movie speak, kid. No one's buying it.

DEAN: I don't care what you're buying. Did you ever stop to think of that? Ingrid, Lauren, Casa Blanca, the woman behind the man, loyalty, responsibility... Who cares? What difference does it make? That was then and this is now and what we were is what we are and nobody cares. We're dead! We're history! The story's been told until no one listens any more. They're not interested. We're not even interested. The King is dead! Long live the King!

BOGIE: You had me going for a moment. You almost said something. You edged right up to it like you were going to jump and then it slipped away like a fat rainbow trout. You had your fingers on it but it slipped away.

DEAN: What are you talking about? It's like a bad script – all words and no content. No guts! You're fishing in a cesspool and all you can come up with is crap! There's nothing there! It's empty, used up, dead and forgotten!

BOGIE: Dead? Yes. Forgotten? No. There's something there. Something nobody knows but us. Something we kept hidden from everyone but ourselves – maybe even ourselves. That's what we have to get at. We've got to dig until we do. Otherwise...

DEAN: Otherwise what?

BOGIE: Otherwise we'll never blow this joint. We'll be stuck here till the end of time.

DEAN: We are stuck here! Don't you get it? This is it, daddyo! It's all we get!

BOGIE: I don't believe that, kid, and neither do you.

DEAN: It doesn't matter what we believe. You're not the boss! You're not the tough guy. You're just another big shot who ended up in the dust heap on the boulevard of broken dreams. We're stuck! End of story.

BOGIE: You'd like that, wouldn't you? Nice and clean. Turn off the lights and hit the road. No more scenes and no more cuts. The trouble is: We don't have final say on this one, kid. There's no more writers, directors or agents to tidy it all up. All we have is the truth buried beneath legends that each of us had a hand in creating. You're right about one thing: The story is written. The Hollywood version is in the can. The one that sells old movies and memorabilia. The one that makes us all more valuable dead than we were alive. We can't touch that one but we can tell the truth. That is if we've got the guts.

DEAN: What makes you think they got it wrong?

BOGIE: In your case, kid, you. You're hiding something. That was a part of your mystique. Blondie here too. Now that I've had a chance to look at you day after day, month after month, year after year, I know you're hiding something. I don't what it is and I don't know why but sure as I'm sitting here you're hiding something.

[BLONDIE bursts into tears and walks away.]

COUNTRY: Damn it, Boge. Lay off. I told you this would happen.

[BOGIE rises and crosses to Blondie.]

BOGIE: I know how you feel, sweetheart, believe me. And you know how I feel about it. It's important to me. I believe it's important to all of us but if you want me to back off just say so. I will.

BLONDIE: [through tears] No, I don't want you to back off. Really. It's just that...well, you're hitting pretty close to home.

BOGIE: It's the same for all of us, sweetheart. Peel away the legend and let's see what's left. What's behind that pretty face and all that Hollywood hocus-pocus?

BLONDIE: What if, after you're done peeling, there's nothing left?

BOGIE: There's got to be, sweetheart. I can't be wrong

about that. [gazing into her eyes] You're as deep as the seven seas.

BLONDIE: I'm not so sure. Norma Jean died a long time ago. I spent years looking for her. She was gone, Bogie. Vanished. It's as if she never existed.

BOGIE: I don't believe that and deep down neither do you. Why bother to hide something that isn't real? And you are hiding something. We all are. Or were. I've told you my secret. I was in love with two women. I let one of them down. The one that needed me most of all. I'm not ashamed to say it. I was scared. It wouldn't do for a tough guy to admit he was afraid to walk down that path of the unknown with the woman he loves. I didn't have the guts to stand up for her. So you've heard my story. Now it's time I heard yours. All of you.

The kid here died in a car crash. Headin' down the highway at a hundred and twenty per. Did you know what you were doing? Did you write the end to your own script? Country boy chucked it all with a bottle of downers. Why? What's the story behind the story? Then there's you, sweetheart, the greatest mystery of them all. Who did you call that night and what did he say and why do I know it was a man? Questions. The stuff of legends. Only we have the answers. Who goes first? Country?

[COUNTRY finds busy work, DEAN stares into his cup, BLONDIE sits at the counter.]

COUNTRY: Don't look at me, I'm just a soda jerk.
BOGIE: Dean?
DEAN: You're not my father.
BOGIE: Right. If I was I'd give you a slap across the chops that'd send you halfway to China. What about you, Blondie?
BLONDIE: I can't, Boge. I'd like to but I can't.

BOGIE: All right. I never thought it'd be easy. It's something we're all going to have to face and we face it tonight. I didn't know that until just a little while ago. Now I do. That's the way it is. It's clouding our vision and poisoning our minds. There's something in the air and it has to be cleared up now or it'll choke us to death.

DEAN: That's a good one.

BOGIE: Oh, I know you think this is all there is, that you just go on wallowing in your own pity, whining and mumbling into your cup of java. But there's more to it than that. Open your eyes and you'll see it clear as crystal. Dead? Yes but we're here for a reason.

DEAN: Yeah?

BOGIE: Yeah.

DEAN: How is it that you're the one who sees it all, Bogie? What makes you the privileged one? What makes you the big shot?

BOGIE: Good question. The answer is simple: I'm not the only one who sees it. Blondie sees it. She's all but said so. Country sees it, too. He just doesn't want to upset anyone. You? Who can tell? You're the best when it comes to hiding the truth. You've worked it into an artform.

DEAN: It's called acting.

BOGIE: Depends on how you look at it. To me acting was always about peeling away the layers of deception until you expose the heart of the matter. The truth.

DEAN: Sure but it's also selecting which truths you want to expose.

BOGIE: Fascinating concept. You were quite the actress, Blondie. Should have won an Oscar or two. If you weren't so beautiful maybe you would have. People in the biz could never look past that beauty to the talent under the surface. What do you say?

BLONDIE: There's a fine line between acting and living. I would have been a better actress, I think, if I'd have revealed more of myself, if I'd have let Norma Jean back in.

But they didn't want to see it. They always wanted Marilyn. I wanted to be loved so I gave them what they wanted.

BOGIE: The Misfits?

BLONDIE: I was drugged. I could hardly stand up.

BOGIE: You were beautiful, Blondie. The scene where they rounded up the horses brought tears to my eyes. Drugs or not, that was acting. You didn't hold back. [turns to Dean] Then there's that scene in East of Eden where you take your frustrations out on your poor old father. That was acting. I'm not saying this to make you feel good. We all know what it's like to let our honest to God feelings out on stage or in front of a camera. Even Country had his moments. The irony is we were all so bad at it in real life.

DEAN: I don't see where this is leading. We did what we were supposed to do. We did what they wanted us to do and they paid us to do. So what?

BOGIE: That's right. We all got so good at playing our public images we forgot how to be ourselves. You were always the angry young man, on the edge, fighting windmills, cursing the moon, swinging your fists at thin air. Always fighting, always struggling and never knowing the whys and what for. The real Dean knew what he wanted. He wanted acting and he got it. He wanted fame and glory and he got it. He wanted fast cars, pretty women and a lot of money in his pocket. He got it all. Sound familiar, Country? It gets better. Just as he gets everything he always wanted, he drives his car into a tree at a hundred and twenty per. He cashes his chips, says goodbye to Hollywood and checks in to never-never land. Why? Because it really wasn't what he wanted after all. He wanted something more or something different – something that he couldn't get.

DEAN: It was an accident.

BOGIE: Don't pull that one with us, kid. We know better. There are no accidents. A choice was made. You made that choice. No one made it for you.

DEAN: All right. So I could have lived. I could have been crippled with a limp. I didn't want to live that way. So what?

BOGIE: Bullshit, kid, you drove into that tree with intent. You ended it just as surely as if you held a gun to your head and pulled the trigger. Only then there wouldn't have been any doubt. No mystery, no legend.

DEAN: I had it all. Three films and I had it all. It takes most actors a lifetime and they still don't reach what I had in three pictures. [waits] I always knew how to make an entrance and an exit. They'll be talking about me in a hundred years! I'll live forever.

BOGIE: Forever's a long time, kid. We're all legends here. Look where it's gotten us.

DEAN: It's good enough for me, pal. What more could I have done? What else was there? I did it all, had it all. I was on top of the game. There was nowhere to go but down.

BOGIE: So you ended up here. The land of the legends. A rundown café on the Boulevard of Broken Dreams.

DEAN: Yeah, what of it?

BOGIE: Why not somewhere else? Why not somewhere more fitting for a man who's seen and done it all? Why not Paradise? Why not some fancy city with fast cars and pretty women?

DEAN: I like it here.

BOGIE: How's that, kid?

DEAN: This is where I belong.

COUNTRY: I'm with Dean, Boge. We've got to accept it and make the best of the way things are.

BLONDIE: I like it here, too. I love you guys. But Bogie's right. There's something missing. We can't accept the way things are. We'll never be happy if we do.

BOGIE: Thanks, Blondie, I knew I could count on you.

COUNTRY: Of course you can count on her.

BOGIE: What are you trying to say, Country? Spit it out. Get it off your chest.

COUNTRY: Any fool can see she's in love with you. Sorry, Blondie. We all know. It's time we got it out in the open.

BOGIE: That's right. Get it all out. [to Blondie] You love me and I love you. But I've left two loves behind. That's where my loyalties are. A man can't forget that sort of thing. If he does he's no longer a man. He's not worthy of love. I have to settle my account just as you do with Joe and Artie.

BLONDIE: They left me behind long ago.

BOGIE: Maybe so. Still, you've got to talk to them. You've got to come to an understanding before...

BLONDIE: Before what, Bogie?

BOGIE: Before we can move on. That's what it's about. We've got to move on. So what's it going to take? How can I convince you that it's no more use hiding the deep, dark secrets?

BLONDIE: It takes understanding. We all accept each other as we are but we can't understand each other until it's all out in the open. We're afraid. We're afraid that if we do let it out, if we let the world see us as we really are, they won't accept us anymore. They won't love us, Boge.

BOGIE: You can't love someone you don't really know. You can pretend, sure. Maybe it works for a while but sooner or later you've got to find out what's inside. Until you do love is just a game. Something to pass the time. Like the movies.

BLONDIE: [waits] All right, I'll talk.

COUNTRY: Priscilla did it.

BOGIE: What's that, Country?

COUNTRY: Priscilla. She done me in.

BOGIE: [waits] Looks like you're off the hook for now, sweetheart. Country's got a story to tell.

COUNTRY: She poisoned me. She poisoned my mind and then she poisoned my body. She done me in, Bogie. I

loved her. Hell, I still love her but she done me in.
BOGIE: Well, well, the first revelation of the evening. Congratulations, kid. I'm proud of you.

[BLONDIE goes to Country behind the counter, comforts him as he sobs.]

BLONDIE: You poor dear. There, there, let it out. [He regains control and she leads him around the counter to sit.] Come on now. You sit down while I pour you a nice cup of coffee.
BOGIE: Feels better, doesn't it? Feels like a freight car's been lifted off your shoulders.
COUNTRY: Guess so. I've been carrying that one around a long time.
BOGIE: Tell us about it.
COUNTRY: [shrugs] Who knows? Might do me some good.
BOGIE: Now you're talking. [to Dean] Listen up, kid. Might do you some good too.
DEAN: Get off me, man. I'm listening.
COUNTRY: She was such a sweet young thing. Always did like 'em young. They just seemed so tender and innocent. That's what Silla was to me. I don't think it was there in the beginning. The poison, that is. Can't say for sure. Never was much at judging folks. If it was there I sure didn't see it.
DEAN: They never show you their claws until they've got 'em sunk in your heart.
COUNTRY: Yeah. Well, we had us a good old time. Took her everywhere she wanted to go whenever she wanted. Bought her everything she looked at twice. The Colonel said I spoiled that gal. Maybe I did. When I finally settled down and brung her back to Memphis that's when I first saw the change. Silla was bored. Being with me wasn't enough for her any more. She wanted high times, rock and roll with the

big boys – Mick and Johnny and the like. I tried for a while but I couldn't keep up. My career was sidetracked. The big boys and the pretty people stopped inviting us to their parties. After that I saw less and less of Silla. I know she was cheating. I blamed myself. I begun to realize I was on a downward spiral – heading nowhere fast. That's when she left me. I ended up going off to Vegas where I could pretend I was still the King. Started hitting the booze and the pills real heavy.

The day I died something funny was going on. Silla was there that day. I hadn't seen her more than once or twice in years. She told me she'd found someone new – someone who knew how to treat a gal like her. Then she went off and had a talk with the Colonel. He never did say what it was all about. Just that she was concerned about me. I noticed a new prescription come in from Doc. I should have known right there. The Colonel and the Doc was in on it. Seems they come to the conclusion I was worth more dead than alive. They kept playing my favorite songs – mostly gospel – and filling my drinks and feeding me pills. Next thing you know I'm walking down the boulevard. Had no idea what happened to me. Except now I'm dead. Took me years, replaying that night over and over, before I realized what it was: Silla. She done me in.

[Lights fade.]

END ACT ONE.

ACT TWO

(As before: BLONDIE consoles COUNTRY.)

BLONDIE: You only hurt the ones you love.
COUNTRY: You think so?
BLONDIE: That's what they say. I say you only hurt the ones that love you. It seems to me you're better off.
COUNTRY: Maybe so. Maybe that's why I don't mind being here, Bogie. I like you folks. I don't have to be the King. I don't have to be no one. I can just be me.
BOGIE: Good for you, Country. That's what it's all about. Being yourself. Now there's nothing to hold you back. Unfortunately, the way I see it, we're all in this together. We're only as strong as the weakest link. Blondie's ready to talk. That leaves you, kid. What about it? You want to listen to the lady or are you ready to spill the beans?
DEAN: [mumbling] I'll talk.
BOGIE: What's that?
DEAN: I'll talk! Just give me a minute.
BOGIE: Take your time. Take all the time you need. We've got all night. Of course, I'd like to get this settled before the new kid arrives. If he's going with us, we'll have to work fast. No time for excess baggage. Say Country, how's about fixing us up for another round? [looks at Dean, still staring into his coffee] Looks like we may need it.
COUNTRY: Sure, Boge.
BOGIE: Country tells me the new kid was quite the musician. Whadya know?
BLONDIE: I only know what Country told me. He started a band called The Beatles. They were the rage until they broke up. Had something to do with his wife.

COUNTRY: Yoko.

BLONDIE: Yeah. He was heavy into drugs and booze until he settled down in New York. Raised his kids. Everything was looking up. He was writing and recording again. He was healthy and happy. That's when some crazy kid gunned him down on the street.

COUNTRY: [motions to a paper on the counter] It's all in the paper if you want to read it.

BOGIE: Thanks. Maybe later. He doesn't seem like our type, does he?

BLONDIE: No. Then again, what is our type? Country didn't seem our type when he got here. Maybe he's hiding something too.

BOGIE: Could be. Seems everyone has something to hide. [glancing at Dean] Maybe he hated his father. Still, I hope they know what they're doing. A new arrival at this stage doesn't seem right.

BLONDIE: Maybe there's more.

BOGIE: That's what I'm afraid of. Hey Country, you're not holding out on us, are you?

COUNTRY: Gee, Boge. I don't think so. I loved my daddy. He was a good old boy. A little rough maybe but I liked him.

BLONDIE: Maybe we're just scratching the surface. Conscious guilt. The face of shame. Maybe we have to get down to the subconscious – the deep dark places we've never allowed anyone to see – not even ourselves.

BOGIE: Christ, this could take centuries.

BLONDIE: Tell me, Bogie: Would that be so bad? Staying here with me, with us?

BOGIE: No, sweetheart, it wouldn't be so bad. Not as long as we stay on the path. Not as long as we're still moving forward. It's standing still that drives me crazy. The feeling that we're stuck. We can't move forward and we can't go back.

BLONDIE: [moving to him] It's awfully nice to hear you say that, Boge. I was beginning to think you didn't like me.

BOGIE: Sweetheart, there's not a man alive who doesn't like you. I've tried to make you understand the situation. Once the air is cleared it's a whole new ballgame.

BLONDIE: [smiles] Good. I like ballplayers.

BOGIE: I know you do. So what was he like?

BLONDIE: Sweet. He was a *real* sweetheart. Sometimes no one's to blame when it doesn't work out. It was like that for me and Joe. He was jealous. He couldn't help it. He could never understand the movie business. He couldn't accept that it was my job to be sexy and attractive – not just to him but to every man. Not just in the movies but all the time. We started having trouble in bed. That's when I knew. We both knew it was over.

BOGIE: I see. I hope you don't mind my asking.

BLONDIE: Not at all, baby. You can ask me anything.

BOGIE: Thanks, kid. But first we've got to get back to the business at hand. If we let him off the hook now we might never get him back. How about it, Dean? By my count you've been staring into your coffee for over twenty-five years. Seems you should have thought it through by now. Frontward, backward and sideways.

DEAN: Back off, Bogie!

BOGIE: I'm through backing off, kid. I've been backing off ever since I found you wandering the boulevard, head down, hunched shoulders, collar up, looking like the dog who just ate his master's slipper. I know it's not easy. Take a lesson from Country here. The woman he loved, honored and respected knocked him off with a bottle of pills. How bad could it be?

DEAN: I said I'd tell you about it and I will. Just…don't push me.

BOGIE: You don't want to be pushed? Come clean. Get it over. Just a little suggestion: Start in the beginning and let it roll.

DEAN: The beginning? All right. I hated my father. You got that right. The son of a bitch had a habit of beating up women. My mother just took it. She took it and took it and took some more until I was old enough to take it for her. He thought it was funny. Beating the crap out of his own son. Then one day I turned the tables on him. Knocked the son of a bitch right on his ass. I can still see that shit-eating grin on his face. The bastard liked it. I walked out and never looked back.

BOGIE: Good for you, kid. He got what was coming to him.

DEAN: It took me years to figure out what he'd done to me. I guess I blocked it out. He...he...he...

BOGIE: It's okay, kid. We get the picture. He...abused you.

DEAN: [tears] I loved him!

BLONDIE: [comforts him] I'm sorry. I know. I know.

BOGIE: That's enough, Blondie.

BLONDIE: How can you be so insensitive? I thought you cared about him.

BOGIE: I do. Believe me, I'm touched. But the kid's still got a story to tell. If he doesn't tell it now it may be years. It may be never. Leave him be. Let him stand on his own two feet and tell it like it is.

DEAN: He's right. I've got to talk. [pulls himself together, stands, paces] You've got it about half right. I was on top of the world. Had everything I wanted. Mostly I just wanted to be an actor – a real actor. I never wanted the movies. But that's what actors do. Go to Hollywood, make some movies, put some money in the bank and go back to the stage. That's what I should have done. That was the plan. I never wanted to be a star. It just...happened. All of sudden all these people are following me around. What do you think about Ike? What do you do with your free time? Who do you hang with? What kind of cologne do you wear? I didn't have a private life any more. I'm an open book.

I loved making movies. I loved East of Eden and Rebel without a Cause. I loved playing the underdog, the troubled son of middle class parents. I loved how the kids all dug it and dug me. I wanted to be the next Brando. Then came Giant. It was a chance to prove myself as an actor. Playing the same character over a thirty-year lifespan. I pulled it off. I proved what I was worth as an actor. I was not just another Hollywood pretty boy. I was an actor!

BOGIE: [waits] That's all very nice, kid. You wanted to be an actor. You were an actor. I tip my hat to you and I'm not one to tip my hat to anyone. But there's still something missing, kid. What happened? What changed what should have been your crowning achievement into a heap of crumpled metal out on a deserted road?

DEAN: [intense] You want to know what happened? You really want to know?

BOGIE: Yes, I do. We all do.

DEAN: I found out something. I found out who I was, what I was and I couldn't face it.

BOGIE: What was it, kid?

DEAN: [tears] A fucking fruitcake! All right? I was a fruitcake, a fag, a fop, a goddamned queer! All right? Are you satisfied? Are you happy now?

BOGIE: [waits] Ecstatic. You don't realize it yet but you just freed yourself of a terrible burden you've carried for too long. Listen, kid, it's not that big a deal. The closets of Hollywood are full of men who like men. They didn't let it get in their way. They did their jobs. Sure you might have lost a few jobs if it leaked but you'd have gained as much as you lost. You might have been a god.

DEAN: I didn't want to be a god! I wanted to be left alone!

BOGIE: Who knows why we make the choices we make? But we have no choice when it comes to things like that. You are the way you are because you were born that way. It's nothing to be ashamed of.

BLONDIE: [to Dean] Maybe that's why I've always felt so close to you. You remind me of one of my dearest friends: Montgomery. He was the only person I knew who was more screwed up than I was. We understood each other. We didn't have to say anything. We knew. I loved Monty like I love you.

DEAN: You're a real sweetheart, Blondie.

BOGIE: Isn't she?

BLONDIE: You know...that may be why I loved Joe so much – even after it was over. I always wondered why he didn't find someone after me. There were a lot of women just waiting for him to look their way. I had a strange feeling about it. Of course Joe would never do anything like that. He couldn't. His fans would never forgive him. He would never forgive himself. Still, deep inside, maybe Joe liked other men. He never talked about his father. Who ever really knows the truth? Even about yourself.

BOGIE: While we're on the subject, do you mind if I ask you something?

DEAN: What's that?

BOGIE: Was it Rock?

DEAN: Yeah. Now you know. That's the whole story.

BOGIE: I thought as much. We all knew about Rock. If you don't mind my saying so, it was obvious. No one gave him a hard time about it. He kept it to himself. That's the way he wanted it. Maybe he didn't have the guts to deal with it and maybe he had reason. Hollywood was famous for turning on its own.

BLONDIE: Rock was a sweet guy. He always went out of his way to help people. He was one of the few guys who didn't have enemies. Everyone liked Rock. If he'd have liked girls I'd have known about it. I might have fallen for him myself.

DEAN: I don't know about all that. All I know is I

didn't have the guts to deal with the situation.

BOGIE: Well, you do now.

DEAN: You're right. I feel better.

BOGIE: Of course you do, kid. The truth will set you free. All these years you suffered under the delusion that the truth would destroy you. It might have, too. Now, it's on your side. No more lies. No more pretense. [waits] Well, sweetheart, it's down to you. How about it?

BLONDIE: Okay. I'm ready. Where do I begin?

BOGIE: In the beginning, sweetheart. In the beginning.

BLONDIE: You want to hear about my childhood?

BOGIE: I don't mean to be insensitive, kid, but you can skip all that. It's an open book. Unless of course there's something we don't know about.

BLONDIE: No, not really. I wasn't abused – neglected but not abused. I don't think we can ever overestimate the impact it has on us. Being tossed around from home to home like an old pair of shoes. A child doesn't understand. I only wanted to be loved.

BOGIE: Forgive me, sweetheart, but I think you're stalling. What's it all about if not the men in your life? Not the first guy. That was a fluke. But the rest of them. Tell me if I'm wrong: Doesn't it begin with Joe?

BLONDIE: It would be easy if that were true. Everything would have been different. At least I think it would have.

BOGIE: I'm stumped. You're not talking about that character who wrote the book. The guy you married down in Mexico and had it annulled a week later?

BLONDIE: [laughs] Heavens, no! That was a part of my charm. I could make a man feel like he was the only one – even when he wasn't. I learned early what a pretty face and a nice figure could do for a girl. I used it. I used it whenever I needed to. Sometimes I'd use it just for a laugh. Put a man in his place and send him packing.

BOGIE: I'm beginning to get the picture.

BLONDIE: Not you, Boge. You're different.

BOGIE: I bet you say that to all the guys.

BLONDIE: I only said it to a few – only when it was true. I understood the difference between sex and love. I knew that you could have good sex without love. I knew that you could have love without sex. I knew how difficult it could be to have both. Why is that, Boge?

BOGIE: You never found the right guy.

BLONDIE: You think so?

BOGIE: I know so. But let's get this train back on the tracks. Where does it begin if not Joe? Who was the first?

BLONDIE: It all began...with Jack.

BOGIE: The prez?

BLONDIE: He was a senator back then. A dashing young prince form Massachusetts. A carefree playboy with the wind in his hair and adventure in his heart. He had a smile that could just melt you. It made you feel all warm and soft inside.

BOGIE: You mean to tell me you were Jack's gal for all those years?

BLONDIE: I was his mistress. Jackie knew. She didn't seem to mind. She was frigid, you know. I wasn't the only one but I was his favorite. We even made love during the campaign. He said he couldn't go on without making love to me. I was worth the risk.

BOGIE: I'll bet you were.

BLONDIE: You're sweet. The question I never asked was: Was he worth the risk to me? An affair with a senator is hard enough to hide. An affair with the president is impossible. We managed to keep it from the public but a husband is something else. That's what broke Joe and I up. I wanted to tell him about Jack. I couldn't do it. I tried to hide it from him. I didn't want to hurt him. But he knew. He didn't know who. Not back then. But he knew there was more to it than my career. Years later I told him the truth. I knew I could trust him. He hated the Kennedy's but he stood by me all those years. He was a true friend. He was the only man who ever earned my trust.

Then came Arthur. My prince. My intellectual and spiritual guide. I thought it was over with Jack. It was for a while. We were happy. He tried to understand. He really did. The President needed me. But Arthur couldn't accept it. That's why I could never blame him. It was too much to expect from any man. Even for me.

BOGIE: That's all very touching, even enlightening. But let's cut to the quick, shall we? Who did it and why?

DEAN: Always pushing! Leave her alone. She either tells us or she doesn't. It's up to her.

COUNTRY: Yeah, Boge. Let her tell it her own way.

BOGIE: Ganging up on me, are you? Sure. She can tell it any way she wants just so long as she tells it.

BLONDIE: Someone else came into the picture. Jack was getting a lot of pressure to end it. The press knew. They just weren't talking. Everyone was afraid of blackmail. That's when I met Bobby. Oh, I'd seen him before. Plenty of times. But he'd always kept his distance. Maybe he was afraid of me or maybe he was afraid of his older brother. Who knows? Jack sent him to talk to me. He said he couldn't trust anyone else. We hit it off right away. He was not like Jack. Jack was always carefree. Nothing seemed to bother him. He was never serious. Bobby was very serious. We talked about acting, politics, psychology, philosophy – everything we cared about. I fell in love with him. He was the first man I'd ever known who treated me like an equal. He actually told me he wanted to marry me – even if it meant his career. [waits] Bobby was there that day.

BOGIE: The day you died.

BLONDIE: That's right. He told me he had to stop seeing me. They were all against me: Jack, Peter, the advisors and politicians. They said I would destroy Camelot. Not just Bobby and Jack but the future of the country. They said I was a danger to the world.

BOGIE: That's a lot of weight on those pretty shoulders.

BLONDIE: It was. I said I understood and I did. I didn't want to but I did. Still, I knew he'd come back. They all come back. Maybe they knew it, too.

BOGIE: But he didn't.

BLONDIE: He never had the chance. [waits] They came after he left. The Italians in suits. Gangster types. At first I thought they were friends of Joe's. Joe was always trying to save me. But they weren't friends. They said all I had to do was take the pills and call Bobby. They said it would save his life. I didn't know what else to do so I took them and I called. I knew he was staying at Peter's but he wouldn't talk to me. He could have saved me but he wouldn't talk to me.

[BLONDIE breaks down; BOGIE comforts her.]

BOGIE: It's entirely possible, sweetheart, that he didn't grasp the full importance of the situation.

BLONDIE: You think so?

BOGIE: I know so. Take it from me, kid, knowing how you felt about him, if he'd have known he'd have done something about it. Maybe it wouldn't have been in time. Maybe it wouldn't have been enough. But he'd have tried. A man doesn't let the woman he loves die without trying to stop it.

BLONDIE: He did love me. I know he did.

BOGIE: Sure, kid. A woman's never wrong about that.

BLONDIE: [brightens] You're right. A woman's never wrong about that.

BOGIE: Let's not get carried away. You done good, kid. Real good. But the evening's still young. We've got plenty ahead of us.

[We hear a drunken JOHN approaching, singing "I am

the Walrus. They watch him outside the windows as he checks for an address. He is dressed in his Sergeant Pepper's costume and carries a bottle. Enters.]

JOHN: Excuse me…aren't you…?
BOGIE: Yes we are. You must be Johnny.
JOHN: Who's Johnny? [sings] I am the Walrus! Koo koo ka choo!

[JOHN takes a drink and collapses on the floor; BOGIE and DEAN pick him up and help him to a seat at the counter; BOGIE hands the bottle to COUNTRY.]

BOGIE: This is going to be tougher than I thought.
DEAN: Dead drunk on his first night. Reminds me of someone.
COUNTRY: He never could hold his booze.
BLONDIE: Poor dear. I know just how he feels.
BOGIE: I guess you do. We all do. Drunken fool. Doesn't even know what happened to him.
JOHN: [coming to] Hey Elvis! The King! How's it hanging?
COUNTRY: I'm fine. A hell of a lot better than you right now.
JOHN: I'm fine. Great. Never better. [flash] They told me you were dead.
BOGIE: They told you right, kid.
JOHN: [to Country] If you don't mind me asking, what's he doing here?
BOGIE: I might just as well ask the same about you.
JOHN: What I mean is: Where's Jimi and Janis and Morrison? They said I was going to meet them.
BOGIE: Curious. You been holding out on us, Country?
COUNTRY: First I heard of it, Boge.
BLONDIE: Who's Jimi and Janis?
JOHN: Have you never heard of Jimi Hendrix? He of

the burning guitar? And Janis Joplin, queen of the rock and soul? And Morrison, the Lizard King? Dark poet of rhythm and blues? Me and Jimi, Janis and Morrison: We're the next generation of legends. We've come to take your place I suppose.

BOGIE: So that's it. That's what they have in mind.

JOHN: I thought they told you. I'm sorry. It's not my doing, you know. I'm just a rock and roll man. I write the songs but I don't have all the answers.

BOGIE: I don't suppose you do. Whadya know? We're being evicted.

JOHN: Not all of you. The King stays. That's what they told me anyhow.

BOGIE: Well, well, whadya know? Country stays and the rest of us are out on the streets. Whadya think, Country?

COUNTRY: I'd just as soon stick with you folks. Nobody asked me.

BOGIE: I'll miss ya, kid. We all will. We've grown to appreciate your down home kindness. You've been a great help to us. The question that remains is: Why? Why are we still here? Why did they want us to greet Johnny as if he was one of us? Why not clear the deck? Then there's the question of where we're going and if we're going together.

JOHN: If you don't mind my asking: What have you been up to all these years?

BOGIE: Not much, kid. Not much. Right now we've got more important things to think about.

BLONDIE: Wait. Maybe that's it. Maybe that's why we're still here. So we can explain it to him. Tell him what we've learned so he can carry it forward.

BOGIE: You may be on to something, Blondie. Not like a welcoming committee. Not to give him the layout. Country can do that better than we can. What Country can't tell him – or won't because he's such a gentleman – are the things we talked about tonight. We've got to share them so

JACK RANDOM

John here can follow our example and get on with his life.

JOHN: I don't have the foggiest idea what you're talking about but I sure would like a drink if you don't mind. I'm dead and I'd like to get drunk.

COUNTRY: [pours and hands him a cup of coffee] There you go, John, a nice cup of coffee.

JOHN: What's happened to you, Elvis?

COUNTRY: Call me Country.

JOHN: I'll call you whatever I like. It's not fitting for the King of Rock and Roll to be pushing cups of coffee behind a fucking counter.

COUNTRY: Things are different up here.

JOHN: I'll say and you can call me the Walrus if you don't mind.

COUNTRY: Okay, Mr. Walrus. I do it because I don't mind doing it. I like it. Keeps me busy.

JOHN: You're sure about that?

COUNTRY: Sure I'm sure.

JOHN: No one forced you into it?

COUNTRY: No sir, I just sort of took to it.

JOHN: You're absolutely certain?

COUNTRY: Believe me, nobody here does anything they don't want to do.

JOHN: All right then. It just doesn't seem right.

BOGIE: Be that as it may, Blondie here has an idea that we ought to tell you what we've learned. She thinks you might benefit from our knowledge.

JOHN: That's what she thinks. What do you think?

BOGIE: I think maybe she's right. We ought to talk.

JOHN: What if I don't want to talk? I've been talking all me life. Look where it's got me.

BOGIE: And I thought Dean was a tough one.

JOHN: Don't mind me. It's just the way I was born. You want to talk, I'll listen. I'm good at it. I really am. And if I fall through a crack now and then, just let it pass and we'll get along fine.

BOGIE: Right. Well then, let's get started. The fact is we each have something to share with you. A secret. Something no one downstairs knows about. If I'm right, you might have something to share with us.

JOHN: Not likely. My life is an open book – as if anyone really cares.

DEAN: [mumbles] That's what I said.

JOHN: What's that?

BOGIE: Get used to it. He mumbles a lot and he doesn't like repeating himself. He came through tonight though. He spoke loud and clear. We're proud of him. Ain't that right, Country?

COUNTRY: That's right, Boge.

BOGIE: Blondie?

BLONDIE: That's right. He showed some courage.

BOGIE: He told us the truth about his suicide.

JOHN: Suicide? They told me you crashed in a blaze of glory! We stopped by the roadside in California just to read the marker. Said it was a tragedy.

BOGIE: That's the story they want you to believe. We know the truth. We've learned it tonight. Say kid, do you want to tell him?

DEAN: No Boge, you go ahead.

BOGIE: I guess twice in one night is too much to ask. The fact is the kid found out he wasn't exactly your regular kind of guy. The fact is he had a thing with Rock Hudson. He couldn't accept it. So he drove his car at a hundred and twenty per straight into a tree.

DEAN: A rock.

BOGIE: That's right. A rock. How's that for suitable?

JOHN: A bit extreme, don't you think? I once had a thing for Paul.

BOGIE: Who's Paul?

JOHN: Me partner in the band. We started The Beatles. I got drunk and told him I wanted to bugger him. I don't think he liked it much. I mean, he was flattered, who wouldn't be? But he didn't want to be buggered. Maybe that's when the trouble started. Everyone thought it was Yoko. It wasn't Yoko. It was me. I couldn't help the way I felt about him. I just wanted to hold him and kiss him. He was always such a pretty boy. He told me to get off his back – more than a figure of speech, that one.

BOGIE: Well I'll be.

JOHN: What else have you got?

BOGIE: Not much I guess. Things must have changed since we were around. Things must have changed since Hollywood kicked an actress out of town for having a child out of wedlock.

JOHN: They have indeed.

BOGIE: Well, you've seen Casa Blanca, haven't you?

JOHN: A classic. Who hasn't?

BOGIE: That's good. I'm glad to hear it. Well, the fact is I was in love with Ingrid.

JOHN: So was I. So what?

BOGIE: No, not in the movies, kid. In real life. I loved her and she loved me. But I was afraid for my career, afraid of what Hollywood might do. Later, when she needed support from her friends, I turned my back. I didn't have the guts to face it.

JOHN: Shocking.

BOGIE: Yes it is. I've come to terms with now but it hasn't been easy. It won't be settled until I've had a chance to talk with her face to face.

JOHN: What would that settle? I've been in love with six or seven women at a time throughout me entire life. Never the same ones. I like a variety. I mean, let's face it: Yoko was beautiful on the inside but on the outside... I needed more. I turned me back on all of them. I talked with some of them afterwards. It doesn't change a thing. It's a nice gesture, like please and thank you, but it doesn't change a thing.

RANDOM PLAYS

BOGIE: Just the same, that's how I feel about it.

JOHN: Have it your way then. Was there anything else you wanted to unburden yourselves?

BOGIE: Country here was killed by his wife.

JOHN: I'm not surprised. She was a pretty little thing, wasn't she?

COUNTRY: Prettiest thing I ever laid eyes on.

JOHN: You and half a dozen others I happen to know. It was Yoko who did me in. Did you know that?

COUNTRY: We was told you was gunned down by a crazed assassin.

JOHN: I saw him in the apartment three weeks before it came down. I noticed him because he looked at me with a strange expression. I asked Yoko about him. Said he was a friend from the old days. Yoko put him up to it. She was jealous. Not about me love affairs but as an artist. She didn't want me coming back and stealing the show.

DEAN: Doesn't that bother you?

JOHN: It bothers me a great deal. I had plans. I was a father you know. Still, she did it with flare. I'm grateful for that much. God knows I probably deserved it. And she waited until I was done with Double Fantasy. I'm grateful for that as well.

[BLONDIE starts laughing.]

BOGIE: I don't suppose you had an affair with Queen of England?

JOHN: Can't say that I did. Have you seen the old bat?

BOGIE: Blondie here had an affair with the President of the United States for what? A decade?

BLONDIE: Longer.

BOGIE: Right through two broken marriages. Maybe you've heard of him: John F. Kennedy.

JOHN: Of course. The fallen prince of Camelot.

BOGIE: She ended up falling in love with his little brother, Bobby. And Bobby fell in love with her.

JOHN: A great man, Bobby. Would have stopped the war if they hadn't killed him.

BOGIE: Bobby was there the night she died. He left just before the mafia boys came in to do their dirty work. Maybe they wanted to pin it on Bobby. Who knows? What we do know is that she called Bobby. Had he answered he could have come to her rescue but he turned his back.

JOHN: That is a strange one. I had a premonition about me own death. I can't explain it. I called George to tell him I thought Yoko was about to do me in. I asked if I could come stay with him. He said he wasn't in town. I told him I didn't care. "I'll jump on a flight and meet you in Tibet or fucking Bangladesh if I have to. I just don't want to go home." He told me to sleep it off and that was that. I loved that man. He could have saved me life but he didn't take me seriously.

BOGIE: Well, I'll be.

JOHN: I guess I've got one on all of you then.

BLONDIE: I guess you do.

JOHN: But I ask you: Is that what it's all about?

BOGIE: Whadya mean?

JOHN: I mean maybe we should just get on with it, you know? Forget about the past. It's over and done with. Believe me they've already forgotten about us. It's the legends they remember. The pictures, the movies, the songs and the stories. They could care less about the people behind it all.

BLONDIE: He's got a point, Bogie.

COUNTRY: We've been trying to tell him that for years.

DEAN: He's just too stubborn to listen.

JOHN: Maybe you're both right. You can't leave the past behind if you're still hung up on it.

BOGIE: Sure. We had to do what we had to do. That much is clear. Now that it's done maybe it's time to go on.

RANDOM PLAYS

Whadya say, Blondie?

BLONDIE: That would suit me fine, Boge.

BOGIE: All right then. That's just what we'll do. Country, call us a cab, will ya?

COUNTRY: Sure, Boge. [pops a nickel in the pay phone on the wall and calls...]

BOGIE: [to Dean] Say kid, you're welcome to come along with us. We'd be pleased to have you.

BLONDIE: Of course we would.

DEAN: Thanks but I think I'll strike out on my own. Wander down that boulevard and see what I can see. Maybe someone will take me in.

BOGIE: Sure they will and maybe it's best. You've been under my wing for too long. Time to get some fresh air. Gather some new experiences. Maybe you'll find what you're looking for.

DEAN: Doesn't matter as long as I'm looking.

BOGIE: That's the ticket. As long as we keep moving we'll be okay.

COUNTRY: Cab's on its way, Boge.

BOGIE: Fine. We'll wait outside.

[JOHN pulls a bundle of letters out of his jacket and distributes them.]

JOHN: I almost forgot. They handed me these at the gate. I think there's one for each of you.

BOGIE: Whadya know? Messages from downstairs.

BLONDIE: How do they do that?

BOGIE: Beats me. Why do they always do it at the perfect time? Let's have a sit, shall we?

[Everyone sits and reads; JOHN grabs the paper.]

JOHN: Is that all they've got to say about me? "Former

Beatle. The intellectual half of the famous Lennon and McCartney songwriting team." What about Imagine? What about Double Fantasy?

COUNTRY: Let it go, John. I was just a country boy who struck it big on the Ed Sullivan show.

JOHN: Right. [waits] Who's it from?

COUNTRY: Silla.

JOHN: Read it aloud, can't you? No more secrets.

BLONDIE: I'd like to hear it.

BOGIE: So would I.

DEAN: Same here.

[Lights fade; spot up on COUNTRY.]

COUNTRY: All right. Here goes. "Dear Elvis: I know I did you wrong. I know you can never forgive me for it. I won't ask you. I just want you to know that it wasn't you. My eyes were filled with stars and I wanted more than you could give. I couldn't stand still and watch your career go down hill. I know you did your best for me. I loved you for it. But I loved money and fast cars and Hollywood parties too. I got what I wanted but I pay for it every day and every night. I know now that I'll never stop paying for it. Please, Elvis, you don't have to forgive me, just forget. I wasn't worth it. I'm not worth it now. Give your tender love to some who deserves you. Yours, Priscilla."

[Lights up.]

BOGIE: That about wraps it up for her, hey Country?

COUNTRY: Yeah, I guess it does.

BOGIE: Mine is from Lauren.

[Lights fade; spot up on BOGIE.]

"Dear Bogie: How could I ever forget about you?

Wherever you are, whatever you're doing, my thoughts are with you always. I just want you to know that even though I haven't remarried, I've gotten on with my life. My life is rich and full of love. I have the deep satisfaction I still get from stage appearances and the occasional film. I've won two Tony's and I'm doing quite well financially. I hope that you have also gotten on with it. You were always so loyal. It's hard for you to let go of the things you love. Well, let go, Bogie. Love and kisses, Lauren. P.S. I had a long talk with Ingrid a while back. Believe me, she knew how you felt about her. We both did. She has no regrets. She wishes you nothing but the best."

[Lights up.]

BOGIE: Well, I'll be. They knew. All this time.
DEAN: I guess it's my turn.

[Lights fade; spot up on DEAN.]

"Dear James: I don't know if this will reach you but if it does I want you to know that the feelings we had were mutual. I'm sorry things turned out as they did for you. I never wanted to see you hurt. That's why I thought it best to turn away from it. I should have known. You have to confront these things face to face. A lot has changed since you've been gone. There's more acceptance now. Maybe things could have been different. There's also a terrible disease that no one understands. It seems to feed on shame and fear and ignorance. It has laid claim on my life. I'm not long for this world. I'm an old man now who's facing his dying days and the time has come for me to ask forgiveness of a lot of people. After all these years you are at the top of the list. Forgive me, Rock."

JACK RANDOM

[Lights up.]

DEAN: You're forgiven, Rock.

[Lights fade; spot up on MARILYN.]

MARILYN: "Dear Marilyn: Please believe me when I say I didn't know. I didn't know they were going to kill you. I would have come – even if it placed my own life in danger. I would have taken care of you. But I didn't know. I'd love to see you sometime if only for old time's sake. Jack would love to see you, too. He didn't care for you like I did but he did care. In another world and another time maybe we could have been great lovers. We might have had a nest full of children and lived happy ever after. Unfortunately, we landed in the world we did, with all its glories and its many flaws. Things never turn out quite like you want them to. The word here is you've found someone new, someone special and loyal, someone who loves you very deeply. I want to wish you all the happiness you can find. No one deserves it more than you do. Yours with love, Bobby."

[Lights up.]

BLONDIE: There it is. Mine didn't have to travel far – just across town.
BOGIE: Let's stop by on our way out, shall we?
BLONDIE: I'd like that. Could we?
BOGIE: Anything you say, sweetheart. It's time someone took care of you like you deserve to be taken care of. Your father should have told you: Never trust a politician.
BLONDIE: I didn't have a father.
BOGIE: That's right.
BLONDIE: Bobby told me.
BOGIE: He was right ... and he was a politician.

RANDOM PLAYS

[Sound of a cab pulling up, honking.]

BOGIE: Looks like our ride is here.
COUNTRY: Sure am going to miss you folks.
BOGIE: You know how we feel. You take care of yourself.
COUNTRY: I will. I promise.
BLONDIE: Maybe now you'll play your music.
JOHN: We'll insist on it.
COUNTRY: Thanks, John.
DEAN: [rises, head down, moving back and forth, almost as if in pain; crosses and embraces them each in turn] Like Country said, I'll miss you guys.
BLONDIE: I'll miss you too, Dean. We'll keep in touch.
DEAN: I'd like that.
BOGIE: Sure, kid, if they let us. We don't know where we're going or where we're staying but if it's possible we'll drop a postcard by the café. Come and see us. Any time.
DEAN: Sure, Boge. I will.
BOGIE: I'll miss you not being around to spar with. Just one thing, kid: Stop mumbling.
DEAN: [mumbling] All right, Boge. Sure.

[Cab honks]

BOGIE: Hold your horses! Say Country, how's about a round for the occasion?
COUNTRY: You've got it, Boge.

[COUNTRY serves drinks around.]

JOHN: Before you shove off, I want you to know: I made it all up.

BOGIE: Made what up?
JOHN: All that stuff about the girls I had and the thing with Paul and George. It's a pack of lies. I don't know what came over me.

[BOGIE, BLONDIE, DEAN and COUNTRY look at each other and break out laughing.]

BOGIE: Sure, kid, we knew it all along.
JOHN: You don't believe me. I can tell.
BOGIE: Sure we believe you.
BLONDIE: I believe you.
COUNTRY: Same here.
DEAN: [smiles] I believed every word of it.
JOHN: Seems there's one in every crowd. Ah well, I guess it doesn't matter.

[They raise their cups in a toast]

BOGIE: Here's looking at you, kids!

[Freeze. Lights out.]

END ACT TWO.

GERONIMO'S REVENGE

SETTING

An adobe structure with thick walls, fallen into disuse. Near the borders of New Mexico, old Mexico and Arizona at the base of the Chiricahua Mountains, it was once a way station, trading post and saloon for travelers from Tombstone, Tucson, El Paso and other old west towns.

The interior is a large room with a stairwell to unseen sleeping quarters. There is a wooden bar stage left, a wood stove up center and cabinets on the upstage wall. There are several round wooden tables and chairs. Apache and old west memorabilia are on the walls. A wooden sign above the bar reads: Geronimo's Revenge. There is a window off stage right and an entryway down right.

The play takes place in a single night, sunset to morning.

CHARACTERS

DI-YIN: The ghost of Geronimo.
JACK: Mixed breed art teacher from California.
MARY: Mixed breed artist.
JOAQUIN: The ghost of Joaquin Terrazas, Apache killer.
MILLIE: Chiricahua elder.

ACT ONE

SCENE ONE

(SOUND: An owl hoots in the darkness, followed by a chant: Oyah ho hoyay, Oyah ho hoyah. Chant continues under. Spot up on the face of DI-YIN.)

DI-YIN: Oh Great Spirit, hear my plea! I am lost within my land. I am lost within my home. I am lost within myself. I remember the ways of my ancestors but Oh Great Spirit let me be wise.

[Chant continues as DI-YIN spreads pollen in the four directions.]

Oh Great Spirit, hear my cry! I listen to the wind. I watch for the signs. I plant my feet upon the earth but Oh Great Spirit let me be wise.

[Chant fades. Lights up on the area behind the bar, revealing portraits of the great Apache leaders: Geronimo, Mangas Colorado, Victorio and Cochise. The brilliant light of a desert sunset filters in from the western windows. Off stage voices.]

JACK: [off] Don't go in there!
MARY: What? Are you kidding? This is the desert, Jack! [knocks on door] If you want to walk to Agua Prieta, go ahead!
JACK: It's abandoned.
MARY: Somebody lives here! It's clean!
JACK: Nobody lives here but scorpions and rattlesnakes!

JACK RANDOM

[MARY nudges the door open, enters cautiously.]

MARY: Anybody home? [looks around] Come on in, Jack. No scorpions, no snakes, [aside] no cajones.
JACK: [enters] I heard that.
MARY: Look at this place!
JACK: Anybody here?
MARY: I asked already.

[MARY is drawn to the bar; JACK focuses on the stairs.]

MARY: Geronimo, Mangas Colorado, Victorio, Cochise: this is the Apache hall of fame!
JACK: [moves quickly to Mary at the bar, whispers] Mary, keep it down. I thought I heard something.
MARY: That's the sound of your teeth chattering. There's no one here.
JACK: Someone owns this place. It's clean. They're probably upstairs right now. They're just waking up from a long night. I know these desert rats. They're born with a gun in their hand and an itch to use it.
MARY: This is a bar! It happens to be an Apache bar and we're customers. If someone is upstairs, they'll be happy to see us. They're not going to shoot paying customers!
JACK: From the looks of it, this place used to be a bar back when Geronimo drove his Cadillac. Now it's in ruins.
MARY: Let's say you're right. It used to be a bar but now it's not. Where does that leave us? In an hour it'll be dark. Our car is broke down and we're in the middle of the desert. What do you suggest we do?
JACK: [whispers] Just give me a minute. I'll go upstairs and check it out.

[JACK slips upstairs. Sound of a fake scuffle. He emerges, clutching his side and stumbling downstairs where he falls face first on the floor and trembles, going still.]

MARY: [watching unaffected] You weasel!

[JACK remains still. MARY goes behind the bar, pours a shot of whiskey and drinks.]

MARY: Jesus! This *is* Geronimo's Revenge! Ah-roo-uh-roo! Ah-roo-uh-roooo! [clearing her throat] Huh! Huh! Huh! You want one?
JACK: [rising, staring at Mary] I used to be able to fool you.
MARY: You used to be better at it.
JACK: They got any beer?
MARY: [locates a six-pack under the bar] Warm Mexican cerveza. I don't think it's their specialty. Wait, what is this? Tiswin?
JACK: [moving to her] What? No kidding! [takes a bottle, opens it] This is Apache beer! It's made from corn. [drinks] Not bad. Want some?
MARY: No thanks. I've got my own. [opens a bottle, drinks] Tastes like tumbleweed juice.
JACK: Yeah, not bad.
MARY: Go easy on it, mestizo. The night is young.
JACK: Right.
MARY: Jack?
JACK: Yeah?
MARY: Doesn't it strike you as strange they left the door open?
JACK: Out here? Nothing strikes me as strange. These are desert folks. Everyone leaves the door open. They don't believe anyone would just walk in and rip them off.

[DI-YIN gives an Apache war cry – Ai-yai-yai-yai-yai! – that sends JACK and MARY into a panic. Jack jumps the bar and pulls Mary down behind it. DI-YIN enters. His dress is a mixture of traditional Apache and pindah – white man. He wears a red bandana, an old army coat, Apache leggings and high, soft-sole moccasins. He has a silver studded belt about his waist with knife and pistol. He draws his Colt .45, sniffs the air and moves to the stairs. JACK and MARY lift their heads above the bar. DI-YIN turns.]

    DI-YIN: Come out with your hands up, pindahs!
    JACK: Hey, take it easy, we were just…
    DI-YIN: No talking. White-eyes talk too much! Mexicanos know better. Come out here where I can see you!

[JACK and MARY emerge, hands up. DI-YIN looks them over, holsters his pistol and walks behind the bar.]

    MARY: We're not thieves.
    DI-YIN: [hangs his belt on a wall hook] I can see that. These old eyes see many things. They see beyond appearances. They tell me you are not what you seem. I tell them: Who is?
    JACK: Our car broke down. It just lost power and died.
    DI-YIN: So you thought you would come in and help yourselves to whatever you want.
    MARY: We'll pay for it. No one was here.
    DI-YIN: I would have done the same.
    JACK: How much do we owe?
    DI-YIN: [gestures to a tip jar] You decide.
    JACK: Let's see. That's two Tiswin and a whiskey.
    DI-YIN: Two whiskeys.
    JACK: Right. [pulls out a twenty, puts it in the tip jar]
    DI-YIN: You are generous. Like a pindah. I remember the first time the blue coats gave us their whiskey. We were like children. We thought: These pindahs are not so bad. They give us firewater and ask nothing in return. Then they took everything we had.

MARY: It's hard to believe that's still going on.
JACK: Look, we're in a jam here. Have you got a phone in this place?

[DI-YIN lights a lantern and hangs it center stage. The blue light of a full moon gradually filters in.]

DI-YIN: No phone, no electricity, no plumbing. Welcome to the reservation!
MARY: I don't mean to be insensitive but how can you live like this?
DI-YIN: My people have always lived like this. We belong to the earth. It is not a bad thing. It is a good thing. You should try it sometime.
JACK: I hate to inconvenience you but maybe you could give us a ride to Agua Prieta. Like I said...
DI-YIN: Agua Prieta is a very long ride on the high desert at night – even with a full moon. The land changes at night. The winds blow hard. Normally I would not hesitate but my horse is tired. She needs to rest.
JACK: Your horse? You don't have a car?
MARY: Welcome to the reservation! Look, I'm sorry, we haven't even asked your name. What's wrong with us?
DI-YIN: The people call me Di-Yin. [pronounced dee-yin]
MARY: Mr. Di-Yin, would it...
DI-YIN: Just Di-Yin. It is an Apache name.
MARY: Of course, Di-Yin, we're in a bind here. Would it be possible to spend the night?
DI-YIN: You will be my guests. I do not often have a chance to speak with people such as you. There is not much traffic on this road. There are blankets, jerky, tiswin, corn cakes. I would be pleased if you would stay.
MARY: We'd love to, thanks.
JACK: Sure. I just didn't want to impose.

DI-YIN: It will only cost twenty dollars.
JACK: That's reasonable.
DI-YIN: Apiece.
JACK: Sure.

[MARY wanders to window downright.]

DI-YIN: At first light, on my word of honor, I will ride to Agua Prieta for help.
MARY: We're in no hurry. I love this land. The smell of mesquite, the cottonwoods, the chalk white mountains, sage... [a coyote yaps in the distance] It has a quiet kind of beauty. Peaceful. Mystical. It almost feels like home.
DI-YIN: [brings out a case of tiswin and places it on the bar] Help yourselves! On the house!

[DI-YIN lights a fire in the woodstove as JACK retrieves his unfinished bottle and sits at a table drinking. MARY breathes in the desert air.]

MARY: I can almost see Geronimo out there riding his spotted pony fast as the wind, silent as a coyote, sneaking into the enemy camp, making off with his bounty. Geronimo, Cochise, Mangas and Compa: They're as much a part of this land as the mountains.
DI-YIN: You are right, pretty lady. The land and its people are one.
JACK: Do you have any cards?
DI-YIN: You like to play cards?
JACK: I can't think of a better way to pass the time.
DI-YIN: [goes to the table where Jack sits, pulls cards and chips from a drawer and sets them on the table] I also like to gamble but I do not have much money.
JACK: You have twenty bucks. [pulls out two twenties] Now you have sixty.
DI-YIN: [smiles] Let's gamble!

RANDOM PLAYS

JACK: [shuffling as Di-Yin sets up the chips] You in, Mary?
MARY: Sure. [retrieves her drink and sits]
JACK: Nickel, dime, quarter, seven card stud, no frills.

[DI-YIN cuts and Jack deals.]

MARY: Is that open to discussion?
JACK: My deal, my rules.
MARY: What about house rules?
DI-YIN: House rules: Seven stud, no frills, Apache style!
JACK: What does that mean?
DI-YIN: You win the first hand, I take your left ear. You win the second hand, I take your other ear. You win the third hand, you don't want to know.

[JACK and MARY laugh but DI-YIN remains stoic though he smiles broadly.]

JACK: You take your gambling seriously.
DI-YIN: I am Apache.
MARY: It's in the blood. Ace of spades bets a nickel. [they play in silence] Well, Di-Yin, now that we're roommates for the night, I'm Mary. This is my husband, Jack. He's known in some circles as Apache Jack.
DI-YIN: You have Apache blood?
JACK: We both do. Great grandmother on my father's side was full-blood Apache. What difference does it make? I was raised in the white world.
DI-YIN: It makes a difference. Two Jacks raise a nickel.
MARY: I wasn't raised in the white world. Hispanic on my father's side, Apache on my mother's. I guess that's why I'm always at war with myself.
DI-YIN: Your great grandfather took an Apache woman.

Probably stole her. It happens all the time. What tribe?

MARY: Mimbres. Jack is Chiricahua.

DI-YIN: [nods] I knew it. I can smell the blood of Colorado and Juan Jose Compa. It is no accident you have come. This is your homeland.

JACK: [throws in his hand] I'm out.

DI-YIN: Did you know that Mangas once killed two Apache in-laws who challenged his right to a Mexican bride?

MARY: I didn't know that.

DI-YIN: It was his third wife. She bore him three daughters. They were good, strong women. One of them became the wife of Cochise.

JACK: [still dealing] Jacks bet.

DI-YIN: Raise a dime.

MARY: Call.

[MARY and DI-YIN lay out their hands.]

JACK: Three Jacks over two aces. Chief wins.

DI-YIN: [collects the pot] I am a warrior and a man of the spirit but I am not a chief.

JACK: It's just a figure of speech.

DI-YIN: Many have made that mistake but they are mostly white men.

JACK: It won't happen again. [passes deck to MARY who passes it to DI-YIN who passes it back to JACK]

MARY: I'll sit this one out.

DI-YIN: House rules. Apache Jack deals. Let's gamble!

MARY: At least we still have our ears. [motions to the display behind the bar] Is that yours?

DI-YIN: That was put there by a pindah who loved the Apache. Not all white eyes are the same. Cochise trusted his dying words to a white man. His name was Jeffords. He was the only pindah Cochise ever trusted.

MARY: Jeffords? Who was he?

DI-YIN: An Indian agent at Apache Pass.

JACK: Pair of deuces bets a nickel.

MARY: What happened to him?

DI-YIN: Cochise swore he would never be harmed by the Chiricahua people. The Apaches held to his word. Jeffords died an old man and was buried in the sacred mountains. There are those who have seen his spirit at the side of the great Mimbres warrior to this day.

MARY: I'll bet they do. I've read about Cochise but it's always a white man's account. I've heard his body was buried in an unknown grave somewhere in the sacred mountains.

DI-YIN: Cochise was the wisest of the Apache warriors. Red Sleeves was the strongest, Victorio was the bravest and Compa was the smartest but the wisest was Cochise. He knew the strength of the blue coats. He never lost a battle but he knew he would lose the war. The best he could hope for his people was to reserve a piece of the sacred mountains. When that battle was lost he called the spirit of death to him. He wanted to die as he had lived: a free man.

JACK: Are we playing cards or what? A pair of nines raises a dime.

DI-YIN: [tosses his cards in] When the blue coats ordered the Mimbres to Canada Alamosa, Cochise was dead within three months. His body still lies in these mountains.

MARY: Deal me in. [to Di-Yin] He died rather than move to Canada Alamosa? Wouldn't it have made more sense to survive and help his people?

DI-YIN: Cochise was a war chief. He pleaded for a just peace but war was in his heart. If he had lived he would have led his people into a war that could only bring suffering. For him there was no other way.

MARY: So he took his own life?

DI-YIN: He did not die by his own hand. He called the spirit of death to him and the spirit took his life. It is not the same. He might have lived a hundred years. He might have put flowers on the grave of Geronimo. But he would not have lived free. So he chose death. He walked into the other world and did not look back.

You wonder why he did not choose a warrior's death? He was tired of fighting. He was tired of spilling the blood of his people when he knew how it would end. His was a noble death. It saved many lives and marked a path for a new beginning.

JACK: Ace high bets.

MARY: I swear to God! Are you listening to the man?

DI-YIN: He listens but he has two minds, two tongues. One speaks of playing cards. The other speaks of a darkness that clouds his spirit. Cochise is your ancestor. You should show respect.

JACK: General Howard is my ancestor too. Look, I know it's popular to rewrite history. I know how distorted the white man's history is but enough is enough. I've heard the stories. You people leave a few things out. Like the Mexicans Cochise tied to a wagon wheel before he set it on fire. Like the lancing and torture of innocent settlers.

DI-YIN: There were no innocent settlers!

JACK: Like the hundreds of whites Cochise killed to avenge his brother's death, including women and children. The Apache are not without sin.

DI-YIN: I have also heard such stories. The white man's history is filled with the red man's savagery. There is some truth to it. But we remember the savagery done to our people, including women and children. Of these we hear very little. It was the Spanish and the Mexicans who invented scalping so they could count the dead and pay bounty. The whites picked it up from them. But the pindahs were less discriminating. They collected body parts and sold them as war trophies! They cut from our bodies ears, eyes, scalps, fingers, toes, penises and vaginas and hung them in their shops for their children to look at. This I swear to you: For every act of savagery the red man inflicted on the whites, the whites inflicted dozens on our people.

JACK: Vengeance is not a virtue.

MARY: Damn it, Jack! We're guests here.

DI-YIN: No! It is good he speaks his mind. It is good even if you choose to turn your back on your own blood.

JACK: [takes a breath] No, you're right. I apologize. It's rude and I'm sorry.

DI-YIN: [nods] It is a beginning. [smiles] Let's gamble!

JACK: Right. Ace high bets. [the game proceeds]

MARY: Call. Show.

JACK: Aces and sevens. Read 'em and weep. [starts to collect]

MARY: Not so fast, mestizo! Two through six! I believe that's your ear at stake. [she collects; JACK shuffles]

DI-YIN: [laughing] Vengeance! The taste is sweet but the digestion is hard. Like Mexican food!

MARY: You have to have a stomach for it.

DI-YIN: The Mexican stomach is as hard as his heart.

JACK: We agree on that.

MARY: Deal the cards, mestizo.

[MARY cuts, JACK deals.]

JACK: First ace bets.

DI-YIN: A nickel.

MARY: What about Red Sleeves?

JACK: Could we talk about something else?

MARY: Sure. You want to talk about baseball? How about those Yankees! Might go all the way this year.

DI-YIN: I love baseball. I remember when the pindahs came to the reservation to teach us their game. Some of my friends said it would not be wise to beat the white eyes at their own game but we did it anyway. We kicked their butts!

JACK: Right, right. Can't we talk about the living instead of the dead? [to Mary] Do you have a problem with

that?
    MARY: I do have a problem with that.
    JACK: You have a lot of problems.
    MARY: By my count just one.
    DI-YIN: Everyone I know is dead.
    [Silence. Periods of silence punctuate the following.]

    JACK: Ace, Queen. [everyone bets]
    MARY: What do you do out here?
    DI-YIN: Hunt rabbits. Rescue strangers.
    MARY: You were out riding today?
    DI-YIN: Every day.
    JACK: Pair of Queens.
    DI-YIN: Bet a dime.
    MARY: Where do you go?
    JACK: Raise a dime.

[MARY folds, DI-YIN calls.]

    DI-YIN: South of the border. Scouting.
    JACK: Down and dirty. [deals last card down]
    MARY: Scouting for what?
    DI-YIN: I'm planning a raid. For old time's sake.

[JACK and MARY laugh; DI-YIN is stoic.]

    DI-YIN: Another dime, mestizo.
    JACK: Another raise.
    DI-YIN: I think you are playing the white man's game. Pindahs are very good at running a bluff. Compa was killed by a white man's bluff. "Come, we will trade! My whiskey for your scalps!" Mangas led his revenge. Hundreds of white eyes paid with their lives. Then Mangas was caught in another bluff. "Come, we will talk peace! We will make a new treaty!" They scalped him before they cut off his head. You would think Cochise would have learned but he also fell

for a white man's bluff. He escaped with three bullets lodged in his back.
JACK: Nice story. You think I'm bluffing? Call me.
DI-YIN: Done. Show.
JACK: [smiles] Aces over sevens! Fully loaded!
DI-YIN: [waits for JACK to go for the pot] Unlike Compa and Mangas and Cochise, Geronimo learned! He did not trust the white man. He could read treachery in the pindah's eyes. [lays out his cards] Straight flush. King high in hearts. [gathers the pot] I have always liked to gamble. Tiswin on the house!

[They grab bottles, drink and play.]

MARY: I'd like to hear about Mangas.
DI-YIN: Red Sleeves?
MARY: Yes. If you don't mind, Jack.
JACK: He'll tell it anyway.
DI-YIN: Mangas was a beast of a man. One hand taller than any other warrior. He had the head and shoulders of a bull, the strength and wisdom of a wolf, and wore his hair down to the small of his back. As a young warrior he traded for a red coat and wore it every day for the rest of his life. He put fear in the hearts of his bravest enemies but he feared no man. He led many raids and fought many battles – first against the Mexicans and then against the blue coats. He was shot seven times but he never fell.

Like all Apaches, Mangas hated the Mexicans. When the blue coats declared war against Mexico, he gave them safe passage through Apacheria. He gave them supplies, told them where to find water and warned them about Mexican traps. When the blue coats won their war they turned on the Apache. They ordered us to release Mexican prisoners. They ordered us to stop raiding and become farmers.

Mangas agreed to their demands. But when gold was

discovered in the sacred mountains and the white miners flooded into Apacheria, Mangas went to the agency. He told them he would lead the miners to a place in the Sierra Madres where the yellow iron ran like a river through the stone. They tied him to a tree and whipped him until his back was as red as his coat. Until that day no man had ever laid hands on Red Sleeves except in friendship. This Mangas could not forgive. He avenged what happened at Pinos Altos. He had wanted only peace but the white eyes betrayed him again and again. His was a bad death and the pindahs lost a friend.

JACK: [has stopped shuffling to listen] I have no doubt Mangas was a great warrior and a brave man. But in the end what legacy does he leave us but vengeance and death? What path forward does he offer us?

DI-YIN: You speak of vengeance as if it is what the black robes call sin. This is the white man speaking. I am not so sure. I believe in justice. I do not believe in sin. If a killing is just, how can it be a sin? To the Apache vengeance is a vow of honor. Had we not taken revenge how many more of our people would have died? Would the Apache still be walking the earth? In the end revenge may have saved the Apache from extinction. You do not wish the end of our people?

JACK: Of course not.

MARY: Jack, I left my coat in the car. It might turn cold. Do you mind?

JACK: No, I'll be right back.

[Exit JACK down right.]

DI-YIN: You would like to tell me something in confidence?

MARY: How did you know?

DI-YIN: We have blankets. There is no need.

MARY: I see. Yes, I wanted to explain something about

Jack. We lost our son a little over a year ago. He was our only child. He was hanging with the wrong crowd and got caught in the crossfire. It was a gang thing and it hit us hard. Ever since then Jack has been on a soul-searching mission. He blames himself. Maybe that's normal but it goes deeper with him. He's always been proud of his heritage. He knows all the legends, the history and the beliefs. Our son would ask him about the old ways and Jack told him a story every night. We think that's why he was hanging out with a gang. He was looking for his tribe.

DI-YIN: I understand.

MARY: Jack would say nobody understands.

DI-YIN: He is wrong. I know what it is to lose a loved one and to feel responsible. I too have suffered. I have lost the few as well as the many.

MARY: You lost your child?

DI-YIN: My children, my wife, my mother. I was away when the Mexicans came to our camp. They killed all our women and children. It felt as though they ripped a hole in my gut, pulled out my intestines and tied me to a tree so that I would die a slow and painful death. But I was more fortunate than others. I found my spirit guide. I had a vision.

MARY: Is that how you recovered?

DI-YIN: I have not recovered but we go on. How is it that you have recovered so well?

MARY: With me it's different. I know it's not my fault. I know Jack's not to blame. It's the world we live in. Most of the time I want to run away and hide, say goodbye to everything and everyone. Go away and live alone in the country or the desert, anywhere. But I know I can't. We have to go on.

DI-YIN: Yes but we must also fight. There is a war within you and within your husband. That war becomes a battle between you. How you choose to fight this war will shape your future and the lives of your children as well.

JACK RANDOM

[Enter JACK with jackets.]

JACK: It's getting cold already. [observes an awkward moment; hands MARY her jacket] What's going on here?
MARY: Not a thing.
DI-YIN: Let's gamble!
JACK: Would you mind if I took a break? Any more hands like the last and our vacation ends here.
DI-YIN: Not my problem.
JACK: [sits at the bar gazing at the portraits] You've told us about the great warrior chiefs, Mangas Colorado, who never lost in battle, and Cochise, who preferred to die rather than live on the reservation. That leaves Geronimo and Victorio. What's the story?
DI-YIN: Victorio! Quick and cunning, he had the spirit of the coyote! When Cochise died it fell to Victorio to move his people to Warm Springs at Canada Alamosa. The Apache always roamed the land, hunting, trading and raiding. Under Victorio we became farmers. The land was good and the earth gave her children good crops and strong animals. But when the white eyes saw what they had done they wanted the land for themselves. Victorio had to move his people to Tularosa where the land was bad and the water was thick and unclear. Life was hard but the people survived. Then they were ordered to move to San Carlos, a dust bowl of wind and sand where only snakes and scorpions survive. A man can only be pushed so far and Victorio had enough! He told his warriors to hide their weapons in the canyons and caves of the sacred mountains. He broke out of San Carlos with three hundred warriors and set fire to every cabin, ranch and coral he could find. This was Victorio's revenge. They killed many, stole horses and cattle, and fought many battles before he surrendered. The blue coats showed respect and allowed him to return to Warm Springs. Later, when they broke their word again and ordered him back to San Carlos,

he raised another army of warriors. They went south into Mexico and a large bounty was placed on his head. They trapped him in a canyon at Tres Castillas in Chihuahua. They fought hard and when the sun fell in the evening sky they sang their death songs. Survivors say Victorio took his own life with his own knife. He denied the enemy the strength of his spirit.

JACK: Some say Victorio was Mexican. How do you know he wasn't?

DI-YIN: I know.

JACK: How? Were you there? The Apaches took a lot of Mexicans captive – men, women and children. They raised them as their own. For all we know, Geronimo was Mexican.

MARY: [pours a whiskey at the bar, drinks] Your ancestors are rolling in their graves!

JACK: For all I know my ancestors might be Mexican!

DI-YIN: Some men believe only what they see, touch, taste or smell. Others see beyond the senses. They have the vision. They see with the eyes of the crow. An Apache is here! [places his fist on his chest] Victorio was Apache! And you, my friend, are more Apache than you believe.

JACK: I believed. If I hadn't believed maybe my son would still be alive. [silence] So you told him.

MARY: Yes. You might be surprised by what he told me. He lost his family – wife, mother and kids.

JACK: [a curious look gives way to a smile] That's the story of Geronimo. [silence] As a young man he married a woman name Alope. She bore three children. He went on a trading mission to Chihuahua and a gang of Sonorans attacked his camp at Janos. Geronimo's mother, his wife and his children were killed. On his way back to the Chiricahua Mountains he had a vision. A voice spoke to him: No gun can ever kill you! Did he tell you? [pops a tiswin at the table, drinks] Tastes like tumbleweed juice! [sits] Let's gamble!

MARY: I'll pass. I have some serious drinking to do. [pops a tiswin, drinks]

DI-YIN: You know the story.

JACK: I should. I've told it often enough. You got the abridged version.

DI-YIN: If I did not like you, little man, I would cut your tongue out and feed it to you in a soup.

JACK: You could try.

DI-YIN: [laughs] More tiswin!

MARY: [breathes in] I love the desert air! I love this land!

[A coyote sounds in the distance.]

JACK: I might have to leave her here. Do you think you can handle it?

DI-YIN: The woman has not been born Di-Yin cannot handle!

JACK: At your age?

DI-YIN: I'll tell you something you don't know, mestizo! Geronimo lived a hundred years and had two women on the day he died!

JACK: Eighty years and I doubt it.

DI-YIN: Who can tell? [crosses down center, takes a broad stance, cups his hands around his mouth and howls] Come, my friends! The moon is full! The spirits of the desert night are alive! They dance and sing in the wind! Come! Join us! Let's howl!

[All howl and yap and sound the Apache war cry. Lights fade.]

END ACT ONE, SCENE ONE.

ACT ONE

SCENE TWO

(SOUND: Distant thunder. A storm approaches. Lights up on JACK and DI-YIN at the poker table. Di-Yin's chips have multiplied. The set is littered with empty tiswin bottles. MARY is upstairs passed out.)

DI-YIN: You know, little man, you are right about one thing.
JACK: What's that?
DI-YIN: Revenge is not the answer. Take my dog and I take your horse. Take my horse and I take your sister. Take my sister and I burn your tipi. Burn my tipi and I kill your brother. Kill my brother and I kill five of your best warriors. It never ends.
JACK: To the Apache it never ends. Vengeance is honor! Without honor life has no meaning. Kill and kill again until the whole world is in mourning.
DI-YIN: I have killed many. For every loved one lost a dozen gave their lives. But not one killing gave me the peace I desired. Not one eased my suffering. The great wheel of life and death turns around and around without end. It had its place but even a very old, very strong people must change. It cannot go on.
JACK: Why not? It's gone on for more than a thousand years. Why not a thousand more?
DI-YIN: A thousand years is not so long.
JACK: It's pretty long.
DI-YIN: Besides, no matter how strong you are there is always someone stronger.

JACK RANDOM

JACK: Like the pindahs?

DI-YIN: The pindahs are like rabbits in a land without coyotes. They multiply until there are rabbits everywhere – more rabbits than arrows to shoot them.

JACK: Where's the killer of enemies when you need him?

DI-YIN: It is not the killer of enemies we need now. It is the Child of the Water. It is he who slays the monster and returns the people to our home.

[SOUND: Thunder louder and close; flashes of lighting.]

JACK: Life Giver comes in the form of rain and lightning. He tells White Painted Woman she will have a child. She must protect the child from Owl Man Giant.

DI-YIN: You speak of your son. Have you avenged his death?

JACK: I intended to. My blood burned and my spirit cried out for vengeance. But they were only kids. Kids with guns but still just kids. They came from broken homes and broken families. They had no bonds and no loyalties to anyone but their own little tribes. [silence] I went to the courthouse to ask the judge to try them as adults. Then I looked at them and saw their rage. I saw their defiance. I saw their pain. I looked at them and I saw my own son. I used to call him my little warrior. [silence] I asked myself: Who should I avenge? My son or myself? Who should I make suffer? The fathers who abandoned them? The mothers? The drug dealers? The police who turned these kids into their enemies? Or myself? I was the one who chose to live in the city. We could have chosen a better neighborhood. We had the money. But I wanted to raise my son with the people. I didn't want to shelter him. [silence] So I walked out – even before Mary testified. I've never explained it to her.

DI-YIN: She is a strong woman, a good woman. She

understands.

JACK: Maybe so but I don't understand. I don't think I ever will.

DI-YIN: [pulls a hunting knife from his legging and slaps it to the table] So kill yourself! Have your revenge! [waits] Why do you hesitate? Are you a coward? No. Your heart knows better than your mind: You are not to blame. Things happen in this life we cannot understand. We go on and trust that the Great Spirit will make it right.

JACK: I don't believe in your Great Spirit. Not any more. The only thing that keeps me going now is Mary. If not for her I'd take you up on your offer.

DI-YIN: [replaces his knife] So you moved away from the city to where the air is cleaner and the great waters soothe your spirit.

JACK: That was the idea. The only problem is it doesn't soothe the spirit; it only numbs the senses.

DI-YIN: It is a very old spirit that returns you to your homeland.

[SOUND: Coyotes. The storm is near, thunder and lightning.]

JACK: We're on our way to Oklahoma, Indian Territory, where our families live.

DI-YIN: It is good to return to the blood – the blood of the family, the blood of the ancestors, the blood of the land. Do you believe in spirits, Jack?

JACK: What kind of spirits?

DI-YIN: [rises, crosses to windows down right] The kind of spirits that live in all things. The spirit of the land, the wind, the rain, the spirit of the coyote, the wolf, the raven, the spirits that live within you and I, the spirit that is your son even now.

JACK: No. [silence] I want to believe but I can't. People

can make up anything they want to ease their pain. Not me. I'll live with my guilt.

DI-YIN: Listen! Not with your ears but with your heart! What do you hear?

JACK: I hear thunder, rain, a coyote and wind.

DI-YIN: Do your hear their voices as they speak to you? They speak of a man with two spirits, two souls, each opposing the other. They speak of a woman who is alone. She mourns her son's death and the loss of her husband. They speak of a man who cannot let go of his grief.

JACK: I hear the rain and thunder. That's all.

DI-YIN: You are too much in love with your suffering. You cannot hear what you will not. [crosses to bar, drinks] There is a spirit in all things. The eight legs, the six legs, the four legs and the two, the mountains, the wind, the rain and the trees. To recognize the spirit of all things within each of us – ourselves, our brothers and sisters, our ancestors and those who will follow – is to receive the spirit's medicine. To understand a spirit is to receive its power.

JACK: Di-Yin? I've been trying to remember what that means. Di-Yin is medicine man. Geronimo was a medicine man.

DI-YIN: Medicine man is a pindah term. We call them spirit guides and healers. Still, you know a lot for a man who has turned his back on his people.

JACK: I know what I know straight up.

[Flurry of thunder and lightning. JOAQUIN appears dressed as a Mexican bandito, black studded sombrero, fancy black pants, decorated boots, a drenched poncho sheltering his gun and ammunition belts, pistols in hand and a large hunting knife holstered at his waste.]

JOAQUIN: Nobody moves! Joaquin is here! [walks toward the stairs; JACK and DI-YIN rise] Stay where you are! Sit! Keep your hands on the table. What is this I smell?

It smells like fish! [moves to the stairs; JACK rises; he points a gun at him without turning] I told you once, pendejo. I have eyes in the back of my head!

[MARY appears at the top of the stairs.]

MARY: What's going on? [freezes]
JOAQUIN: Ahhh, chica! [backs down] Ven aqui, ven aqui! [she complies] What are you afraid of, my dear? Joaquin will not hurt you. I am here to protect you! From who you might ask? [points to Di-Yin] From him!
JACK: Just take our money and go.
JOAQUIN: It's raining, chico. Didn't you notice? [DI-YIN laughs] Is something funny, viejo?
DI-YIN: The Apache have a great admiration for clowns!
JOAQUIN: Who are you, old man? [circles] There is something familiar about that face. What are you? You are not what you seem. [to Mary] Chica! Esta sentado! Aqui!

[MARY sits at the poker table. JOAQUIN holsters his guns, pulls out his knife, grabs a chair and sits at a safe distance. He plays with his knife constantly.]

JOAQUIN: You have a name, viejo?
DI-YIN: I am called Di-Yin.
JOAQUIN: Di-Yin? [laughs] You are a fake and a thief! All you Apache scum are liars! I spit on you! [spits] Chica! Bring me espiritu con gusano! [MARY hunts down a bottle of mescal with worms behind the bar and brings it to him] Muchas gracias, chicita bonita! [opens bottle, drinks, staring at Jack] Well, well, well, this is going to be a long night! Relax! Take a load off! Que? You are scared? What? This? [the knife] I am sorry. I must keep it for protection. I am very good with a knife, viejo!
DI-YIN: I am sure. To a Mexican good with a knife

means hitting the side of barn. To an Apache it means hitting the wing of a fly.

JOAQUIN: [fake laugh] Ha ha! Very funny!

JACK: Look... [hesitates]

JOAQUIN: No, go on, say it! Who knows? It might be important.

JACK: What do you want?

JOAQUIN: Do you have a cigar? [DI-YIN nods] Chica! [snaps his fingers]

DI-YIN: Below Victorio.

[MARY complies, taking note of Di-Yin's gun belt on the wall; takes a cigar from a box, starts back.]

JOAQUIN: Dos! [MARY goes back, gets a second, returns, sits.] Muchas gracias! [lights one with a match; places the second inside his jacket] Ahh, Victorio! That reminds me of a story! You know the story, viejo? How Victorio ran from the white soldiers in Chihuahua. How Joaquin Terrazas tracked him down and killed him like the Apache dog he was. Of course, Victorio was a Mexicano by blood but he was raised an Apache dog and so he was. I like that story: Joaquin! The greatest Apache killer of them all!

What? You are not pleased? Oh, I see, you want to know when I will leave this place? Then you would be happy? Then I will tell you. I will leave when it stops raining. Of course, it may never stop raining. Who can tell? If it does, I will leave. Are we happy now? Are we amigos? There is just one thing: You hurt my feelings. You make me think you do not like my company. Oh yes, even Apache killers have feelings! [blows cigar smoke in the air]

MARY: I apologize.

JOAQUIN: You are very kind, chica, but I must tell you: Chico does not feel the same. [to Jack] So I must ask you, friend: Why don't you just go?

JACK: [waits] Do you mean that?

JOAQUIN: Of course. You are free to go! [JACK and MARY rise and move to the door.] Un momento, por favor! There is a problem. I'm sorry but I do not wish to be alone with him. [points to Di-Yin] You can go, senor, but she must stay.

JACK: Right, we both stay.

JOAQUIN: If you insist.

MARY: Hold on, Jack. You go, I'll stay. I'll be fine.

JOAQUIN: [smiles] I know what you're thinking. You are thinking maybe he can go for help? Yes, that's right. Like el viejo I can read minds. But it is no good. There is no help for this kind of thing. However, if it makes you feel better, if it makes you el hombre grande that you are not afraid to go out in the rain with the thunder crashing and la espiritus de la desierta then go! We'll be fine.

[JACK thinks and sits.]

MARY: Go!

JACK: He's playing with us. If I decide to go he'll change his mind.

JOAQUIN: [playing with knife] I do not like to be called a liar, pendejo! I do not like to repeat myself! If you want to go, then go!

JACK: What if I stayed and Mary left?

JOAQUIN: [thinks] No. Es no bueno. [shrugs] I like her much better than you. We speak the same language.

JACK: Right. We both stay.

JOAQUIN: If you insist.

MARY: What do you want with us?

JOAQUIN: You think this is my idea? You think I want to be here? I have nothing better to do? No, no, think again. I am here because el viejo wants me here. Por que? Maybe he likes me. Maybe he likes to be entertained. Who knows? [laughs; to Di-Yin] They don't believe me. You think the old man is your amigo? I'll tell you what: Let's find out who we are dealing with. Chica: Who are you?

MARY: Mary. Mary Red Hawk Sanchez.

JOAQUIN: What kind of name is this? You are Indio and you are Mexicano.

MARY: My mother is Apache and my father is Latino. It's not uncommon.

JOAQUIN: It is very common. I regret to say that I myself have fathered more than a few Apache dogs. Juan Jose Compa, Victorio, the children of Mangas Colorado and Cochise. Geronimo? Who knows?

DI-YIN: The blood of Geronimo is pure Chiricahua. This I know.

JOAQUIN: How would you know? Were you there, viejo?

DI-YIN: I know.

JOAQUIN: A man knows what he wants to know. It is no matter. [to Mary] Tell me about your Apache name.

JACK: She got it from me. It was the name my grandfather gave me. When I was a boy I saw a great bird in the sky. My grandfather told me it was a hawk. After that all birds were hawks. When I saw a redbird I told him about the red hawk. It became my Indian name.

JOAQUIN: That is a good story. You Apaches have such good stories! We Mexicanos do not have such imaginations. We take the name we are born with but you Indios: Crazy Coyote, Crow Feather, Running Bear, One Who Yawns, Stinking Feet...such imagination! What is your name, viejo?

DI-YIN: I am called Di-Yin.

JOAQUIN: I am not as stupid as you think. That is not a name.

DI-YIN: In the old way, we do not give our names to the enemy.

JOAQUIN: So I am the enemy. You see how it is? It is good to know where we stand. What else, Mary Sanchez?

RANDOM PLAYS

What do you do with your lives?

MARY: I'm an artist. What else do you want to know?

JOAQUIN: Children?

MARY: I had a child. A boy. He's no longer with us.

JOAQUIN: [sincere] I am sorry. I know. You think because I have guns and a knife I have no feelings but I do. I am sorry.

MARY: It happened a long time ago.

JOAQUIN: Still. I understand. I was a father myself. I lost my wife, my son and my daughter to that Apache dog Geronimo!

DI-YIN: That is a lie.

JOAQUIN: How would you know, old man?

DI-YIN: Geronimo never killed women and children.

JOAQUIN: Did I say killed? Oh no, I wish to God he had killed them. He took them and raised them as Apaches. I spent the rest of my days chasing them. So you see, my friends, I know: It is great suffering to lose a child. [waits] How old was he?

JACK: He was eleven. A little man.

JOAQUIN: You have no other children?

MARY: No.

JOAQUIN: Por que? You are a strong, healthy woman.

MARY: We decided not to.

JOAQUIN: I do not understand. You decided?

JACK: We can't have more children.

JOAQUIN: [thinks] So it is *you* who cannot have another child. A woman should have a real man, a man who can give her what she needs! You come with me, chica, and you will have a child by the spring!

MARY: I don't want another child. I don't want to bring a child into a world of sorrow and hatred. If I had it all over I'd live in the desert. I'd have nothing to do with this world.

JOAQUIN: [silence] You blame yourselves?

MARY: I didn't say that. Why should we? These things

happen. Maybe we could have done something to save him but we didn't. It's all in the past.

JOAQUIN: It is natural. You are the parents. It is your job to protect your child.

JACK: It was my job and my failure. Mary never wanted to live in the city. I did. She didn't fill his head with big ideas about honor and belonging and standing up for your tribe. I did. I wanted him to be a warrior so he died a warrior's death. He was eleven.

JOAQUIN: [thinks] It is very confusing. Your son died but he did not dishonor you. It happens. Only a woman mourns this long. A man moves forward. Am I right, viejo?

DI-YIN: No man may judge.

[SOUND: The storm intensifies.]

JOAQUIN: Then let the spirits judge! They are very strong tonight. Who calls them? Is it you, viejo? An old soul calls to his spirit allies. [waits] He does not answer. [waits] Is it you, pendejo? The lost one who needs comfort? Or is it you, chica, the one who is alone and in love with the spirits of this God forsaken land? [rises] Chica! Bring me the old man's gun belt!

[MARY obliges as JOAQUIN moves to a table stage right where he sits waiting. As she approaches he grabs her arm.]

JOAQUIN: You will sit with me. [she complies; he places the belt on the table, removes the knife, examines and sniffs it] Muy bueno! It smells with the blood of Mexicanos! [offers it to Mary who turns] Pendejo, you will bring her drink! [he complies; returns to sit] Come, mi amigos! We will drink to the spirits! [all raise their drinks] L'espiritu de la desierta noche! [all drink; storm rages; chanting and drums]

DI-YIN: The Zuni speak of the desert spirits. They are

called kachinas. These spirits spun their webs in rhythms and chants that worked a powerful spell on the people. The women were especially drawn to them. The kachinas seduced them until there were few left to bear children and give life to the tribe. The elders held a special ceremony to ask the kachinas to return to the to spirit world and leave behind only their likeness. Because the elders were respectful and promised to hold their likenesses in reverence they agreed. From that day forward the Zunis hold a ceremony every year to praise the kachinas and give thanks for sparing their women and allowing their people to survive.

JOAQUIN: That is a good story. Here is another. It is the story of a woman. She is the most beautiful woman of her pueblo. She can marry anyone she chooses. She chooses a good man who will give her children, who will always love and protect her. They have a son who is good and brave and makes them very proud. They are happy. But something happens. A fight on the streets. Bullets are fired. The good son is killed. [pause] The woman mourns her son and the man drifts into himself, into his guilt and sorrow. Soon the woman is alone. The spirits call to her in the night. They promise a new life! They sing to her and she is soothed and comforted. She feels alive. She is tired of being alone. When the spirits call to her she answers: Yes! Yes, I will go with you! She chooses the spirit world and she is happy. [drinks] Glasses! We need glasses and more cerveza and another bottle of mescal! [MARY obliges] You like my story, viejo?

DI-YIN: It is a good story.

JOAQUIN: And you, pendejo? You like the story?

JACK: I prefer the kachinas.

JOAQUIN: [laughs, takes a drink of tiswin, spits] What is this? Coyote piss?

MARY: Tiswin. It's Apache beer.

JOAQUIN: You like this, you drink it. You will bring

me what I ask. Cerveza mas fina de la Mexico! Or I will cut off your husband's little finger. [MARY obliges] And you, chica? Did you like the story?

MARY: What story?

JOAQUIN: She drifts away, my friends. The spirits sing to her. Did you like my story?

MARY: [airy] It's a good story.

JOAQUIN: We are losing her, chico. Can you feel it?

JACK: I've felt every day for the last two years.

JOAQUIN: And you do nothing? You don't care?

JACK: I do.

JOAQUIN: But you do nothing. You let the days go by. You mourn. You count the minutes. You feel sorry for yourself. What kind of man are you?

JACK: It has nothing to do with you.

JOAQUIN: I think it does. Am I not human? Am I not here? [smiles] I think your wife likes me just a little. Is it so, chica?

MARY: Is what so?

JOAQUIN: You like me just a little.

MARY: You're a stranger and a terrorist.

JOAQUIN: Still.

MARY: Not likely.

JOAQUIN: But possible?

MARY: Not possible.

JOAQUIN: She breaks my heart. Por que? I am so nice to you. I treat you better than my dog. Almost as good as my horse. But she is a very good horse.

MARY: We're your captives. It's a little hard to overcome.

JOAQUIN: So that is the problem? And if I set you free? But I warn you: There are many spirits out there. Not all of them are as nice as me. But if you want to go [crosses to door], here is the door.

MARY: Both of us?

JOAQUIN: Both of you.

MARY: You heard him, Jack.

[JACK and MARY quickly grab their things and move to the door. They hesitate and look back at Di-Yin.]

JACK: Will you be okay? [DI-YIN nods]
JOAQUIN: Adios, mi amigos!

[As JACK opens the door a massive bolt of lightning strikes. The storm rages, a coyote howls, an owl hoots and they freeze. He closes the door and they turn back.]

JOAQUIN: [shrugs] I told you.

[Lights fade. End Scene.]

END ACT ONE.

ACT TWO

SCENE ONE

(SOUND: The storm fades under a traditional 4:4 beat of Indian drums, followed by the accompanying chant: Hey-yahnah-yahnah-hey, Hey-yahnah-yahnah-hey... The chant continues under.)

DI-YIN: The earth is my mother; my father is the sky. The wolf is my teacher; coyote is my guide. The crow is my brother; the owl is my eye. The earth is my mother; my father is the sky. [chant fades] The paths are many but the way is one. The land is blessed with many spirits. The journey is safe to those who know the signs.

[Lights up slowly. All is as it was. JACK and MARY turn to confront Joaquin.]

JACK: Who the hell are you?
JOAQUIN: I am Joaquin Terrazas! The greatest Apache killer of all time!
MARY: I thought you said you were named after him.
JOAQUIN: I do not always tell the truth.
JACK: Terrazas died over a hundred years ago.
JOAQUIN: What is a hundred years to the spirit of a man?
JACK: You're both jerking us around! Di-Yin and Joaquin Terrazas? What the hell are you two trying to pull?
JOAQUIN: It's good to see there's a little fight left in you, pendejo! If you keep it up I may have to give you a new name.
JACK: It's been a long night already. Level with us:

What do you want?

JOAQUIN: You are asking me?

JACK: You're the one in charge.

JOAQUIN: You think? He sees and yet he does not see – even when it knocks him down.

DI-YIN: It is the curse of the white eyes. What he cannot reason he cannot understand. What he does not understand does not exist. This is your failing: You are too much of the brain and not enough of the heart. Your spirit is as shallow as the waters of the summer rain.

MARY: We weren't always like this.

JOAQUIN: She speaks.

JACK: Mary, that's enough! These people are strangers. Hell, they're not even strangers. I don't know what they are but I don't like it.

MARY: Whatever they are they aren't strangers. They know who we are and we know them. Maybe it's a dream. Maybe it's a nightmare. I don't know but I know this: How we react makes a difference. Real or unreal, dream or concrete reality, what we do now is who we are.

JOAQUIN: Your wife is much wiser than you. You should listen to her. Come! You are going nowhere! Sit back down. Relax, have another drink, enjoy! Tell us about yourselves.

MARY: I married Jack because he was a spiritual man, a gentle but strong man.

JACK: Don't go there, Mary.

MARY: Or what? You'll leave me? You already left me. We're about as far apart as we can get and still be together. I've got to tell you: there's not a lot to lose.

JACK: Fine. Do what you want. Just don't expect me to pretend it never happened.

JOAQUIN: Drink, pendejo! It will not help but it will not matter as much. [to Mary] You were saying?

MARY: I was saying: Jack was a spiritual man. He

knew who he was and what he believed and it was not the ways of the white man. We went to powwows, we joined the American Indian Church, we supported AIM. Jack went to Wounded Knee in 1973. He walked out with Dennis Banks the last night before they surrendered. That was before I met him and before we had our son. We considered ourselves activists in the movement. We aspired to be warriors. We wanted our son to be a warrior. To this day I have no regrets.

JACK: But I do. It goes back a long way. It's the same question Victorio and Mangas and Geronimo faced: The old ways against the new. The hunter-warrior society against the farmer-gatherer. We change. We become more civilized. We adapt to the world we live in. Geronimo was good at adapting. He was a businessman and in the end he was a farmer. Had he lived today he'd be a movie star like Russell Means! Now that's adaptation.

MARY: Maybe you're right but I'd bet my life Geronimo would never have stopped being a warrior and a spirit guide. He never surrendered and he never abandoned the way of his people.

JACK: He stopped fighting and raiding. He had to stop to survive but he never gave up who he was. He was a man of the spirit. No one can take that away from you.

MARY: Not unless you give it away. He never gave up. That's what matters.

JACK: I need time, Mary.

JOAQUIN: You've had enough time, chico. More than enough.

JACK: What is a hundred years in the spirit of a man?

JOAQUIN: That is good, senor. But time is not your only problem. You are a coward.

JACK: I'm not afraid of you or anyone. [rises defiantly and crosses to the bar]

JOAQUIN: And I am not afraid to cut a line in your pretty wife's face. Don't be stupid.

MARY: Let him! I'm not afraid either.

JOAQUIN: I warn you. This could get very messy. [JACK returns to the table, sits] A wise decision, pendejo. It is not something I would enjoy but I am a man of my word and you misunderstand. A man is not a coward because he fears. A brave man is often afraid. It is the man who runs from his fears and pretends not to be afraid who is a coward. This is why the Apache must stand his ground when he hears the hoot of an owl. Nothing strikes fear in the heart of a warrior like that sound. Is it not so, viejo?

DI-YIN: It is so.

JOAQUIN: That is why I learned to make that sound. I would hoot like an owl when we had them surrounded. The Apache are brave but they are not so smart. We Mexicanos run from our enemies but we do not run from our fears.

JACK: Okay, Terrazas, what do you fear?

JOAQUIN: Same things as you. Evil, guilt, the worm of conscience. [drinks the worm of mescal, slams the bottle down] Maria! Do you mind if I call you Maria? [MARY shrugs] Bueno! Mas, por favor! Another worm for the soul!

MARY: [delivers a bottle] If you fear evil why would you choose to serve evil?

JOAQUIN: You are mistaken.

MARY: You kill women and children.

JOAQUIN: To avenge my people. This is not evil. What do you think, viejo?

DI-YIN: A man cannot judge another on these matters. It is not the man who chooses the spirit of the night. The spirit chooses the man.

JACK: Vengeance is the root of evil. Darkness can't enter the soul of a man free of vengeance.

DI-YIN: Perhaps it is so. Still, what man can judge? What is evil to the pindahs may not be to the Apache. What is evil to the Apache may not be to the Mexicanos. It is not the deed but the heart of a man that counts. No one can see into a man's heart but the man himself.

MARY: And the woman he loves. Or the woman who loves him. I used to see into your heart, Jack. Now I only see smoke, clouds and confusion. I don't even know you any more.

JACK: You know me. I'm still me. I'm the same man I was before I got lost.

DI-YIN: The spirit of a man does not change. It grows or it dies. It becomes lost in a world it does not understand. The man becomes bitter, angry and vengeful but the spirit, the soul, the center of a man is like a rock. It can only be shaped by the running waters of time.

MARY: Then the running waters have changed you. You're not the man you were. You've changed.

JACK: [shrugs] I've always been between worlds. I am the mestizo! I embraced my Apache blood. It became my religion and my cause. But I never let go of the white man's way. I like money. I like convenience. I don't want to hunt for my food. I like restaurants and grocery stores and computers and movies. I don't want the blood of my enemy. I want the police to protect me and the courts to hand out justice. Does that make me a hypocrite? [drinks]

DI-YIN: These things you speak of are like fleas to a dog, leaves to the wind, a candle to the great fire of the sun! A warrior does not thirst for the blood of his enemy and the Apache have always had their own police and courts. If you take pleasure in pleasant things it does not make you a hypocrite. It makes you human. That is all.

MARY: You know what I can't forgive? You left me sitting in that courtroom to face our son's killers alone. You have no idea what that feels like. I stared at your back as you walked out without a word. My heart rose to my throat when the judge asked where you were going. I made an excuse – a family emergency. He asked if you intended to testify. I told him I didn't know. You could have cut the silence with a knife. When I got home and asked you why, you said, "I can't explain." There are a lot of things in life that don't require an explanation – forgetting to take the garbage out, getting drunk at a party or looking at a pretty girl on the beach. This was different and you had nothing to say. That's when you left me and that's what I can't forgive.

JACK: I'm sorry.

MARY: Of course you are. Like water for chocolate. I've been waiting two years for an explanation and you say you're sorry.

JACK: I've tried to explain it to you more times than you can imagine. I keep trying even though I know there's nothing I can say that would satisfy you. It would only feed your bitterness, your resentment and your disgust. Yeah, I feel it. I wear it like a blanket of sweat. It suffocates me.

MARY: I promise you: it could be worse.

JACK: Really? Fine. For what it's worth I wish I'd have stayed but I can't change what happened. I walked out because, when I looked at those boys, I didn't see killers. I didn't see someone I could hate. Hell, they didn't even know who pulled the trigger! It was a turf war. It was tribalism. It was the Navaho and the Apache, the Lakota and Cheyenne, the Arapaho and Comanche. They weren't thugs. It wasn't about drugs or money. It was about brotherhood and belonging. They were young warriors doing what their father's taught them. They were just like Jack. I no longer wanted revenge. It felt like a lynching and I didn't want any part of it.

MARY: So that's what you thought? A lynching? And I thought it was about justice! When someone kills your son you're supposed to do something about it. I don't give a damn how young they were. They killed our son!

JACK: [quietly] Jack would have done the same.

MARY: The hell he would have! He was my son as well as yours and he was nothing like those punks! He never touched a gun. We taught him to respect others. He would not have taken another life!

JACK RANDOM

JACK: Really? You knew him so well? You think he never touched a gun? He had one hidden away in his closet. I took it from him.

MARY: [stunned] Why didn't you tell me?

JACK: I promised him.

MARY: What about your promise to be honest with me?

JACK: He begged me not to tell you. He knew how you felt. He promised not to get another gun and in exchange I promised not to tell you.

MARY: You should have.

DI-YIN: [waits] A warrior treats his enemy with respect. We pray that he will be strong and brave for then he will speak well of us in the next world.

JOAQUIN: I am sure that is a great comfort as you take his scalp and still he lives to watch you slice off his cajones.

DI-YIN: It is the Mexicanos who are experts at such things. It is the Spanish who offered bounties on the scalps of the Apache.

JOAQUIN: [shrugs] It is true. We do not pretend to respect our enemies. We punish those who kill our sons and we have no mercy.

MARY: I wanted them to suffer. I wanted them to go to jail. I didn't want to cut off their balls.

JOAQUIN: [reaches out and runs his fingers across her cheek] You are soft as a woman should be. [Mary does not move; he rises and displays his knife as he moves behind her] Pendejo? You allow your woman to speak to you this way? [grabs her hair with one hand, presses the knife to her throat with the other] I would cut out her tongue!

JACK: We aren't animals. We don't dominate and control our mates.

JOAQUIN: You are wrong. We are animals and like animals we have needs. We must have what we need or we shrink. We have desires and if we are strong we take what we desire. [pulls her hair back and kisses her; she does not respond; he stares at Jack and sits; she pours and drinks]

JACK: Just say the word, Mary.

MARY: Forget it. It's nothing. Less than nothing. It's a fly or a mosquito. It's nothing.

JOAQUIN: [laughs as the storm builds outside] Ahhh, the spirits are aroused. Escuche, mi amiga, escuche!

DI-YIN: The warrior must know when to act and when to wait. He must have the patience of the coyote and the strength of the wolf. His time will come.

MARY: [becoming entranced] Jack?

JACK: Yes?

MARY: I understand.

[SOUND: An owl nearby as the storm builds.]

JACK: Do you?

MARY: I forgive you.

JACK: I never wanted your forgiveness. I wanted you to blame me. I blame myself. The shame and the guilt are my only comfort.

[SOUND: Fluttering wings of crows. MARY rises and goes to the windows.]

JOAQUIN: Escuche, Maria! The spirits call! Go to them! You cannot resist!

MARY: Can you hear them?

JACK: Hear what?

[SOUND: A murder of crows. JACK rises.]

JOAQUIN: Stay where you are, pendejo! Where she goes you cannot follow. [he freezes]

MARY: Can you hear them?

JOAQUIN: Yes, I hear them. The spirits dance for you tonight! Listen! They sing for you!

MARY: Jack?

JACK: I'm here, what is it?

MARY: Crows! There are thousands of them! They're everywhere! They block out the moon! Can you see them? [covers her ears and drops to her knees but is soon mesmerized as the sound transitions to ethereal muse] It's changing. Shadows in the moonlight, beings of light, translucent, beautiful light beings dancing across the sky! They're singing without words. It's beautiful! I feel so safe, so warm, so comforted. They're angels! They're protecting us, Jack. [suddenly disturbed] No, no, no!

JACK: What is it?

MARY: It's Jackie! He's there! He was always such a beautiful boy. He's saying something. He's calling me. He wants me to join him.

[DI-YIN rises, moves upstage.]

JOAQUIN: Where are you going, viejo?

DI-YIN: There is something I must do. Shoot if you must!

[DI-YIN goes to a cabinet as JOAQUIN cocks his pistol and aims. DI-YIN turns around with a bundle of sage, lights it and begins to chant. JOAQUIN holsters his gun.]

JOAQUIN: You and your superstitions!

[DI-YIN spreads the smoke of sage as he chants. He tips over the table where JACK sits, smokes him with sage as he rises. Jack is stunned.]

DI-YIN: Do you accept my counsel?

JACK: What's going on?

DI-YIN: There is no time. Do you accept my counsel?

[JOAQUIN creeps to behind Mary, knife in hand.]

MARY: I feel so light. It's as if I could step out of my body and fly!
[SOUND: An owl hoots as the storm rages. The following dialogue overlaps.]

JOAQUIN: You can!
JACK: I accept your counsel!
JOAQUIN: Believe and you can!
DI-YIN: Do as I do. Speak as I speak. [drops to his knees, hands and eyes to the heavens; JACK does the same]
MARY: They're coming for me.
DI-YIN: Oh Great Spirit!
JACK: Oh Great Spirit!
JOAQUIN: They welcome you, Maria! They call to you!
DI-YIN: We are humble before you.
JACK: We are humble before you.
JOAQUIN: They want you to sing with them, dance and fly in the cool night wind!
DI-YIN: We call upon our spirit allies!
JACK: We call upon our spirit allies!
JOAQUIN: Your son needs his mother's love!
DI-YIN: We call upon the medicine of the crow!
JACK: We call upon the medicine of the crow!
JOAQUIN: They reach out for you!
DI-YIN: To quiet the thunder and confine our enemies!
JACK: To quiet the thunder and confine our enemies!

[MARY raises her hand.]

JOAQUIN: Yes, take his hand!

[SOUND: Storm abates and gradually subsides.]

DI-YIN: We call upon the medicine of the hawk!
JACK: We call upon the medicine of the hawk!

[JOAQUIN places his left hand on Mary's shoulder, places his knife on her throat. She doe not respond.]

DI-YIN: To carry a message of healing!
JACK: To carry a message of healing!
JOAQUIN: Take his hand!

[MARY hesitates, hand still open.]

DI-YIN: We call upon the medicine of the dragonfly!
JACK: We call upon the medicine of the dragonfly!
JOAQUIN: Now, Maria! You must go with him!
DI-YIN: To unweave this dream!
JACK: To unweave this dream!
JOAQUIN: Now, Maria!
DI-YIN: And reveal the true faces of the spirits before her!
JACK: And reveal the true faces of the spirits before her!
JOAQUIN: Now, Maria! The time is now!
DI-YIN: In the name of our ancestors, Mitakuye Oyasin, let it be so.
JACK: I the name of our ancestors, Mitakuye Oyasin, let it be so.

[DI-YIN bows in silent prayer. JACK does the same. Suddenly MARY screams. The spell is broken. JACK goes to her as she collapses. JOAQUIN shakes his head and goes back for a drink.]

JOAQUIN: Oh, Maria, you were almost free!

[SOUND: The storm gives way to gentle rain.

RANDOM PLAYS

JOAQUIN drinks, DI-YIN prays and JACK comforts MARY as she regains consciousness. Lights fade.]

END ACT TWO, SCENE ONE.

ACT TWO

SCENE TWO

(SOUND: Gentle rain. JOAQUIN sits back to the bar, bottle in hand, drinking, Di-Yin's gun belt beside him. JACK comforts MARY, draped in an Indian blanket at a center-left table. DI-YIN has righted the overturned table and sits calmly.)

JACK: What happened? Are you okay?
MARY: [still dazed] I saw something dark, hideous looking, its yellow eyes staring at me and laughing. It crawled under my skin and I knew it was death. It grabbed me and pulled me in but I knew it was evil and I fought back.
JACK: [to Joaquin] Is that it? Is that what all this was about? Scaring us? I think we've had enough.
JOAQUIN: Oh no, senor. I don't think so. You have paid nothing. Your wife has paid for you. She pays for your guilt, your cowardice, your shame. Is it over? I don't think so. You must pay.
JACK: You want my blood? You want my life? Take it but leave my wife alone!
JOAQUIN: I feel for you, pendejo. I see you are sincere. I wish I could help. I really do. But you are asking the wrong man.
JACK: [to Di-Yin] What's going on? Is this your doing? Is it witchcraft, a spell, a charm?
DI-YIN: It is all of these things. We have raised the spirits of the Chiricahua Mountains, the spirits of the desert night, the kachinas who still walk the earth: They are all very real as any man knows who has traveled this land. If you are asking: Am I responsible? Then I must tell you I do

not command the spirit world any more than I command the wind and the rain. The spirits appear to us because we have something they want.

JACK: What do they want?

DI-YIN: They want your wife.

JACK: Why don't they just take her?

DI-YIN: They cannot. A living being cannot survive in the spirit world – not for long. To go with them she would have to leave her body behind. She would have to give up her life. The spirits will not take her against her will and they will not come again unless she calls them.

MARY: I won't. I wouldn't.

DI-YIN: You remember the story of the kachinas? They are very powerful spirits. They seduce the soul. When you are weak who can tell?

JACK: What would happen if she said yes.

DI-YIN: Terrazas is their ally. He slits her throat and releases her spirit to join them.

JOAQUIN: [laughs, lights a cigar] You believe that? [crosses to windows] You should! [laughs and begins pacing] There is another way, viejo. If we cannot have her spirit at least we can have some fun! For example, I could kill her husband and take his scalp for old times sake! I am sentimental about these things. I might take his cajones but I am told he has none. [laughs]

JACK: I'll tell you again. You want my blood? Go for it! We'll see what happens.

JOAQUIN: Maybe I am mistaken. You are a very brave man. Cajones the size of a bull's. But it is not your blood that interests me, pendejo. It is your wife.

JACK: You'll have to kill me.

MARY: Don't be stupid, Jack. He came by night. He'll leave at first light. We don't need a martyr. We just need to survive the night.

JACK: [to Di-Yin] Is it true?

DI-YIN: When I was a boy my grandfather told me a story.

JOAQUIN: [laughs] You Apache! Everything is a story!

DI-YIN: I was very sick with a fever. My grandfather brought me back from the dead. He told me one day I would be Di-Yin. This is why he told me the story.

[SOUND: Thunder at a distance.]

JOAQUIN: Get on with it, old man! When the spirits return we must be ready.

DI-YIN: It was a long time ago – before the pindahs came to this land. The tribe was touched by the Spanish fever. They had a great healer. He worked his medicines, his spells and his charms. He did not sleep. He prayed night and day. Still he watched his people die. At first it took the old and weak. Then it took the young. It seemed he could do nothing to stop it. On the seventh circle of the sun he called the bravest warriors to counsel. He said the Great Spirit had turned his back on them. They had become too proud. They had turned from the spirit that lives within. They had forgotten him. Now they would have to make a sacrifice to beat the sickness. He called on them to offer themselves for the tribe. That night the warriors sang their death songs. In the morning as they prepared to take their own lives, the healer came to them and announced that the dark cloud had lifted. His medicine regained its power. The sick recovered and grew stronger. The tribe was saved. They already made the sacrifice. It was not their blood that the Great Spirit required. It was their will.

JOAQUIN: That is a strange story, viejo. Does it mean anything at all?

DI-YIN: It is not the act of sacrifice; it is the will to sacrifice. [rises and crosses to the bar; picks up his gun belt and turns toward Jack]

JOAQUIN: What are you doing, viejo?

DI-YIN: Even a man of the spirit cannot judge another man's heart.

[JOAQUIN pulls out his gun and fires upward; DI-YIN is unaffected.]

JOAQUIN: A warning, viejo! Be careful.
DI-YIN: [to Jack] This much I know: You are lost within yourself. You cannot go forward and you cannot go back. If you are Apache, your path is clear.

[JOAQUIN takes aim at Jack, fires and misses.]

DI-YIN: You must avenge the death of your son. If you are not Apache, I cannot advise you. You must choose. The white man's reason cannot help you. It is the choice of your heart.

[JOAQUIN takes aim and fires; misses.]

JACK: Vengeance is not a virtue.
DI-YIN: It is neither right nor wrong. It is the way of the Apache. It will not give you your son's life back. It will not ease the pain. But you will be whole again. You will go on. You will be a man and a warrior.
JOAQUIN: [fires, misses, tosses his pistol aside, grabs the second] I do not know what you have done to my weapon, viejo, but I think maybe your luck runs out.
DI-YIN: You must choose.
JACK: I choose the Apache way!
DI-YIN: Joaquin Terrazas!
JOAQUIN: [looks around] I'm still here, viejo!

[SOUND: Thunder grows louder, lightning flashes. MARY moves to windows, her blanket dropping to the floor.]

DI-YIN: This man challenges you!
JOAQUIN: [laughs, howls] I accept the challenge! Choose your weapon!

[DI-YIN holds the gun belt out to JACK. He chooses the knife.]

DI-YIN: You choose well.
JOAQUIN: Yes. Especially since I removed the bullets!
DI-YIN: I will hold your gun.

[JOAQUIN empties the gun, hands it to Di-Yin.]

MARY: [enthralled] Jack?
JACK: I'm here, Mary.
MARY: I can see them. They're coming.
JACK: Hold on, Mary. It will be over soon.

[DI-YIN gathers sage and medicine bundles.]

JOAQUIN: Yes. Soon you and I will be together and you will know what a real man is!

[JOAQUIN crouches and circles with knife. JACK does the same. We hear crows.]

MARY: I can hear them. Coming closer. It's horrible.

[MARY crouches to the floor. DI-YIN lights sage and draws a circle on the floor. Kneeling before his medicine bundles he begins to chant: Heyuh-heyuh, heyuh-heyuh, heyahnah, heyahnah, heyahnah... The storm grows and the chant takes on the voices of the ancestors with beating drums.]

JOAQUIN: Would you like me to tell you what I am going to do to your wife when you are dead? [JACK lunges and he steps aside; JACK tumbles to the floor, bounces up] I am going to make love to her like she has never made love before! [howls] Oh, pendejo, I wish you could be there!

[Lightning and booming thunder. JACK starts and JOAQUIN pounces. JACK catches his arm and they tumble and roll, JOAQUIN ending on top. His knife poised to strike, JACK holds his arm. The knife lowers as the hoot and fluttering flight of an owl startles JOAQUIN. JACK throws him and they both bounce up, circling.]

JOAQUIN: The old one works his magic. He fools me once. He will not fool me again.
MARY: They're here! They're angels. Beautiful angels! Thousands of them! They're surrounding me. I can feel them inside of me!
JACK: Fight them, Mary. They're not angels. They're dark spirits. Listen to Di-Yin!
MARY: [rising] Jackie?

[SOUND: Coyote yaps, lightning and thunder.]

JOAQUIN: The trickster! I wonder whose side he is on?
JACK: It's not Jackie! It's an illusion! Fight it!
MARY: No, it's not Jackie. It's someone else. He's calling me. It's so warm and comforting.

[MARY rises, holding her hands out. JACK looks to her as JOAQUIN pounces. JACK recovers, throws him back and they circle.]

JOAQUIN: Very good, pendejo! You have some moves!

JACK: Fight him, Mary!

[Caw of a crow; MARY freezes.]

JOAQUIN: Shall I tell you what I did to Alope, viejo? Yes, I was there. I tied her hands and spread her legs! Her children and her mother watched! She fought very hard but then she gave in and she liked it! Yes, she liked it very much! So I cut her throat! I did not take her scalp. She was a pretty girl. I let someone else do it. I have my weaknesses. I liked her.

[JOAQUIN looks at Di-Yin and JACK pounces. They roll and Joaquin's knife bounces away. JACK emerges on top and plunges his knife into Joaquin's chest. The chant stops and the storm recedes. MARY collapses and JACK goes to her.]

DI-YIN: Great Spirit, hear my song! I offer you the breath I breathe, I offer you my soul. I offer you the sacred seed but oh, Great Spirit, let me be wise.

[Lights fade.]

END ACT TWO, SCENE TWO.

ACT TWO

SCENE THREE

(Lights up slowly. Birds sing as morning light filters through the windows. JACK and MARY are upstairs sleeping. There are glasses and bottles on the floor, tables and the bar. A jingle of keys announces the arrival of MILLIE, an elder Chiricahua woman, who enters and surveys the damage.)

MILLIE: Hello? Anyone here?

[We hear the hustle of JACK and MARY getting out of bed and scrambling to get dressed. MILLIE pulls a bucket and cleaning rags from behind the bar as JACK appears at the stairs, partially dressed. He carries a carved wooden flute as if it's a weapon.]

JACK: [calling upstairs] It's okay, Mary! Come on down! [walks in the room, looks around]
MILLIE: Were you planning on playing that?
JACK: No. I didn't realize... Is it yours?
MILLIE: No. It once belonged to a great spirit guide – Di-Yin. That's Apache for healer. [prepares coffee] Are you Chiricahua?
JACK: [nods] Mimbres Chiricahua.
MILLIE: And your wife?
JACK: We're both Apache. Mixed breeds.
MILLIE: I am full blood. There are not many of us left.

[MILLIE pulls out a large trash can and begins picking up and discarding empty bottles. JACK helps. MARY enters fully dressed. MILLIE stops.]

MARY: Hello.
MILLIE: I'm Millie. I take care of this place.
MARY: I'm Mary. Mary Red Hawk. [they shake hands and Millie looks to Jack, who stops cleaning and joins them, shaking hands]
JACK: I'm Jack. Sorry about the mess.
MILLIE: I've seen worse. You must have had quite a party last night.
JACK: I'm not sure how to say this but we had some trouble here last night.
MILLIE: Trouble? Is that what you call it? [brings three coffee mugs to a table] Coffee will be ready soon. Come, sit, tell me all about it. [they sit]
MARY: Well..., there was an old man. He called himself Di-Yin. [MILLIE smiles and nods] At first we thought he was charming. He told stories. We drank and played cards. We were having a good time until the storm rolled in. A man, a Mexican bandito arrived. He was a bad man.
JACK: He claimed to be Joaquin Terrazas, the Apache killer.
MARY: He terrorized us. He held us captive. He insulted and threatened us. I don't know how but Jack got hold of a knife. There was a fight and Jack... killed him. It was right here... on this floor.

[MILLIE nods and gets the coffee, sits.]

MILLIE: It may take time for you to understand what happened. I know. I don't understand it myself. But there was no storm last night. There is no dead body. See for yourself. It was just ... a dream.
MARY: [silence, she examines the floor where Terrazas was killed] It seemed real.

JACK: What can you tell us about Di-Yin?

MILLIE: [smiles] His Apache name was Goyahkla. He was one of the greatest of our spirit walkers. It is said he could stop the sun from rising to escape his enemies. He walked many times in the spirit world. Now he walks the land he loved.

JACK: Goyahkla? That's Geronimo ... and this is Geronimo's revenge.

MILLIE: It was all in your head, my young friends. You have nothing to worry about. It is over.

MARY: What were they? Ghosts?

MILLIE: Ghosts, spirits, kachinas, it does not matter what name you give them. They like this place. They are drawn to it. It is not the first time.

JACK: What is this place?

MILLIE: It was once a trading post. Now it is owned by a white man from Santa Fe. He used to bring his friends here but not any more. He pays me to look after it.

MARY: Is it for sale?

MILLIE: It is. Very cheap.

MARY: Cheap enough for a couple of struggling artists?

MILLIE: Are you artists?

MARY: Yes. Well, we were artists.

JACK: We'll become artists again.

MILLIE: I could call the owner and tell him you are buyers. You could stay here as long as you like. There are many things I would like to share with you.

MARY: Jack?

JACK: Do you want to stay? [she hesitates]

MILLIE: Have no worries. Goyahkla is very fond of you. You would not be here otherwise. He will protect you.

MARY: What about Terrazas?

MILLIE: They were the bitterest of enemies in life. Now they are the best of friends. Joaquin would never hurt you. It would be the end of his friendship with his greatest enemy. Strange, isn't it?

JACK: That's reassuring.

MARY: I'd like to stay.

JACK: We'd like to stay.

MILLIE: [rising] I am pleased. My husband is good company but we like young people. I will make the call. [starts to exit]

JACK: Wait, my car is broken down.

MILLIE: There is nothing wrong with your car. Believe me. I will back soon. [exits]

MARY: [moves to Jack, embraces him] How do you feel, mestizo?

JACK: I can breathe for the first time since I can remember.

MARY: Since Jackie died. I feel his presence. He knows just as we do: We've come home.

[They embrace. Lights fade to black. We hear drums and Di-Yin's chant.]

END ACT TWO.

QUEEN OF THE LONELY HEARTS

A Play in Two Acts

SETTING

A dark, dusky tavern with typical tables and chairs. It is also a waiting room. Men and women sit one to a table. There is a piano/keyboard at which an entertainer sits. There is a bar and a door to the outside world. There is another offstage door.

CHARACTERS

SONNY BOY BLUE: A jazz-blues musician and singer. When not performing a song, he underscores the dialogue.

MS WHITE: A receptionist dressed in the uniform of a nurse. She carries a pen and clipboard.

MICK: A writer and traveler, middle aged.

SALLY: A hard woman, middle aged.

LONELY HEARTS: Jason, Mary, Mr. Gray, Beauty Queen, Joey, Marilyn, George, Liz, Crystal, Dean, Eve, Bill, Diana, Wilson, Marian, Billy, Mary, Chuck, Henry, Joe, Gloria, Jamie, Gladys, David, Joan, Albert, Carl, Victoria, Jack, Boris, Germaine, Bobby, Cheryl, Martha, George, Sara and Rick: Men and women of varied age and description who deliver their stories and fade away. They are played by a cast of 3-4 men and 3-4 women.

ACT ONE

(General lighting fades. Spot up on SONNY BOY BLUE, the entertainer at his keyboard, who improvises on *Vera* from Pink Floyd's *The Wall*.)

SONNY: [singing]
Does anybody here remember Vera Lynn?
Remember how she said that we would meet again some sonny day?
Vera! Vera! What has become of you?
Does anybody else in here feel the way I do?

[Spot stays on SONNY as he continues softly under; spot up on JASON at a table.]

JASON: She was a free spirit. A gypsy queen and the lady of my dreams. She possessed the kind of beauty you can only behold. But don't touch. You can hold her in your arms, you can give her your love and you can borrow hers. But the moment you touch her...she's gone. She was only a dream. I went to visit her once. She was sitting in the living room with a few friends. One special friend. I knew. I knew as soon as I walked in. I saw it in her eyes. She saw my heart breaking in mine. I caused a scene with my accusing glances and sarcastic remarks. She took me aside and told me I had made a promise that I would never be jealous, that when this moment arrived – we both knew it would – I would understand. I swear I never made such a promise but I accepted it as if I had. I accepted it as a challenge to the depth of my love. I measured my love in pain. But I *was* jealous and I did not understand.

JACK RANDOM

[Light fades on JASON.]

SONNY: [singing]
I still recall the way she looked that day
Remember how she made me feel that special way
Vera! Vera! What am I without you?
Just another lonely soul marking another day.

[Spot out on SONNY. General lighting up. MS WHITE enters with clipboard from inside door stage left.]

MS WHITE: Mr. Jones? Mr. Jones?
MR. JONES: [at a table] Yes?
MS WHITE: We'll see you now.
MR. JONES: [rises] Thank you.

[MR. JONES exits stage left. Spot up on MARY at a table.]

MARY: I didn't know how much I loved him. Not then. The world was too exciting and mysterious! It was so full of promise! There were so many men so interested in finding out what treasures I held for them. I wanted to experience everything: gentlemen with soft hands and sensitive eyes – pleading and worshipping eyes, strong men who knew what they wanted and went after it, dark and spiritual men looking for a religious experience with a woman – Mary Magdalene, Madonna, strange men with a secret, older men with knowledge, younger men with energy, simple men with beautiful bodies, beautiful men with simple bodies, artists, businessmen, students, bikers, writers, so many men and I wanted them all. I got what I wanted or thought I wanted. But when I got older there weren't so many men. Only dreams. My dreams are my company now.

[Spot on MARY fades; spot up on MR. GRAY.]

RANDOM PLAYS

MR. GRAY: Twenty-two years. Twenty-two years, 237 days, seven hours, thirty-three minutes. She was my companion, my lover, my heart, my soul and my life. She died of cancer. For three years she was dying and for three years I died with her. She tried to tell me I loved her too much. She said it wasn't healthy to depend on her love. She knew and she tried to save me. No one can tell me they know how it feels to watch your love dying and to secretly wish that you could take her place. How could she leave me? How could God take her from me? There is no God! Or if there is he is a cruel master. She was my life. She was all that was good in me. Now there's nothing left. A shell. A hollow, empty worthless soul. I'm already dead, waiting to be buried at her side.

[Enter MICK from the outside door. He looks around and approaches SALLY at a table.]

MICK: [gestures] Do you mind?
SALLY: Why not? It's a free country.
MICK: What's the story?
SALLY: Whose?
MICK: This place. What's it about?
SALLY: You don't know?
MICK: I've never seen anything like it. Strange.
SALLY: Isn't it.
MICK: What's a girl like you...
SALLY: Cap it, Mac. There aren't any girls like me. I'm one of a kind.
MICK: Is that right?
SALLY: That's right.
MICK: It's a stupid question. I apologize.
SALLY: Forget it. Who cares anyway?
MICK: I do for what it's worth.
SALLY: It aint worth much, believe me.

JACK RANDOM

[Fade lights; spot up on BEAUTY QUEEN.]

QUEEN: I was a knockout. When I walked into a room every man turned his head and every woman hated me. Everyone knew I had my pick. I loved it. I was gorgeous. The world was at my fingertips. Roses, jewelry, designer clothes, mink stoles: ask and it's yours. What a life! But time takes its toll. I still remember the first wrinkle under my eyes, the first gray hair. A little extra makeup, a little hair dye. But nothing can save you from sagging breasts or the extra pounds around the waist and hips. It all happens so quickly. One day I'm a beauty queen and the next I'm a middle-aged woman. I was still attractive but heads no longer turned and hearts no longer broke. It's hard to compete with younger women. No more diamonds for me! Funny: I thought it would never end. Now I'm just another single woman trying to find a good man. It seems they've all been taken.

[Spot out on QUEEN; exits in darkness.]

MS WHITE: [re-enters] Miss Myers?
MARY: I'm here.
MS WHITE: We're ready for you.
MARY: [rising] Thank you.

[Exit MS WHITE and MARY, inside door. Lights shift to general.]

MICK: Where are they going?
SALLY: Where do you think?
MICK: When they come back, what do they say?
SALLY: They don't come back.
MICK: You've got to be kidding!
SALLY: I don't kid. I used to but I don't any more. No

time for it.
MICK: Why do they go?
SALLY: No place else to go.
MICK: I don't get it. Who are these people?

[SONNY plays *Eleanor Rigby* by Paul McCartney.]

SALLY: You really don't know? [he shakes his head] They're the lonely hearts and this is the last stop.
MICK: [sarcastic] Right. Explain it to me.
SALLY: What's to explain?
MICK: How does it work? How did they get here?
SALLY: Like you and me, they just walked in.

[Light shift: Spot up.]

JOEY: I love Marilyn Monroe. Not like a fan. I really love her. Niagara, Bus Stop, Some Like it Hot, Diamonds are a Girls Best Friend, The Misfits. I saw everything she did. She was the ideal woman. Absolute perfection! The shape of her lips, the curve of her hips, her legs, her breasts: perfection. Absolute beauty. Her innocence, her childlike innocence. Her charm, her sensuality…her breasts. Perfect, body and soul! Why couldn't I have been Joe DiMaggio or Arthur Miller? I'd be a happy man today. Just one small parcel of time with Marilyn Monroe! It'd be enough to last a lifetime. And I'd never be lonely.

[Light shift.]

MARILYN: Joe was sweet. Arthur was so smart and sensitive. They were both sensitive men. I never had a father, you know? I was adopted. My mother was a lot like me. She could find a man easily enough. She just couldn't keep him. I don't know why. I do wish I'd have been just a normal girl. Norma Jean. She was pretty but not too pretty. I'd wish I'd grown up in one house in one neighborhood. I wish I'd gone to school in one school. I could have met a boy, settled down, had kids. I always wanted a child. I wish I'd had a father. Joe tried so hard. He was jealous. He couldn't help it. Arthur wanted to save me but I didn't want to be saved. They just didn't understand. No one understood. How could they? I didn't understand myself. I only knew I needed something, something more than they could give. Not money or jewelry. I never wanted money. Love. I needed love. I needed to be loved completely like the father I never had.

[Light shift.]

MICK: I'm not lonely.
SALLY: Right.
MICK: I'm alone. It's not the same.
SALLY: Right.
MICK: Look, if I wanted a woman, all I have to do is snap my fingers. No problem.
SALLY: Right.
MICK: Okay. Maybe it's not that simple. Maybe the problem is: I can't find the right woman. But, hey, you don't belong here any more than I do. What do you say we blow this joint?
SALLY: You think it's that easy?
MICK: Why not?
SALLY: You don't think anyone's tried? Go ahead. It's locked.
MICK: It wasn't locked when I came in.
SALLY: It's locked from the inside, Einstein.
MICK: Who's in charge here?
SALLY: Forget it. Nobody knows and nobody cares.
MICK: Okay. We'll just wait until someone comes in.
SALLY: Right.

MICK: It's been tried.
SALLY: Right.
MICK: So we're stuck here.
SALLY: You can get in but you can't get out. Got it?
MICK: Right.

[Light shift. Spot on GEORGE.]

GEORGE: I've been married to the same woman for thirty-five years – the same spiteful, nagging, manipulative, demeaning, ball-breaking bitch. Excuse my language. It's a miracle. It should be a record. A friend of mine once said: It's a miracle that any two people stay together any more. I guess I should be grateful. The problem is we hate each other. At least there's passion in our lives. Ever see Virginia Woolf? We're it. George and Martha in the flesh! Only there's no love. None. We never loved each other. It was a marriage of convenience. Whose convenience? Not mine. Not hers. Our parents thought it was great. Everyone was so pleased! Except us. We never had children. Thank God! Low sperm count the doctor said. My wife never tires of reminding me. But I thank God or whatever force of nature decides these things. What kind of warped, twisted creature we would have brought into the world boggles the mind. Lonely? Yes. But not alone. We haven't been alone for thirty-five years. Precious little difference that makes!

[Light shift. Spot up on LIZ.]

LIZ: Of all the men I've ever known, intimately, only one ever touched my heart. He was a playboy, a shameless womanizer and a drunk. He spent money like it was toxic. He had to get rid of it. He was a lot like me. No matter what he said or did or didn't say or didn't do, I never for an instant doubted his love. That's why I always took him back. I always knew he'd die first. The curse ran deeper in him than it did in me. I always knew one day he wouldn't bail out in time. He went too far. It was too late to climb back. Still, he was the only man I ever loved, the only man I ever could love and the only man who could love me with all his heart.

[Light shift.]

MICK: Okay. Since we're not going anywhere, we might as well get to know each other.
SALLY: You're only the fifth man who said that to me today.
MICK: In here?
SALLY: Where else?
MICK: What did you say?
SALLY: Beat it, take a hike, get lost, not interested – variations on a theme.
MICK: I'm not like the others.
SALLY: You think you're different?
MICK: The only one of my kind.
SALLY: I've heard that before.
MICK: What are you so mad about?
SALLY: I'm not mad, I'm bitter. There's a difference.
MICK: Right.

[Light shift. Spot up on CRYSTAL.]

CRYSTAL: I got married when I was seventeen. I was just a child and I got pregnant. A child giving birth to a child. That's what happened to my mama, too. My grandma got married when she was fourteen. Things are different now. Men leave. The mothers stay and the babies grow up without a father. I didn't want them to leave. Johnny and Sara. I told them they could live with me as long as they liked but Johnny joined the navy and Sara got married. She got pregnant. [pause] I can't believe it. It's still going on.

Maybe he'll be different. He seems like such a nice guy. My Bo seemed like a nice guy too. My friends say I should find someone new and I know I should. There aren't a lot of men who want an older woman. There are some I know but how can I be sure he won't leave?

[Light shift.]

DEAN: I was in love with speed. I loved danger, risk-taking. I wanted to experience everything that life has to offer. When did I have time for anyone? If I'd have lived, who knows? Maybe I'd have changed. Maybe someone would have come along. I don't know. I only know I was on the move. I had to keep going, faster and farther. No way I could stop. Stop and you die. [reflects] Maybe I was in love with my own image like Narcissus. Maybe I was in love with myself. Maybe I thought I was indestructible, immortal, a god among mortals. Or maybe I knew I'd die young. Maybe that's how it was supposed to be. I got what I wanted.

[Light shift.]

MICK: So all these people...are lonely.
SALLY: You keep this up and someone might accuse you of being perceptive.
MICK: Would that include you?
SALLY: Why would I be an exception?
MICK: I'm an exception. Why not you?
SALLY: I'm here because I'm supposed to be here. As far as I'm concerned, there are no accidents.
MICK: I can't imagine someone like you being lonely.
SALLY: There are a million reasons for being lonely.
MICK: There are a million reasons for being alone but only one for being lonely.

SALLY: Only one?

MICK: That's right.

SALLY: Okay, Mac, I'll bite. What is it?

MICK: Not following your own heart.

SALLY: Mister, you've got a lot to learn.

MICK: You don't think it's possible to be alone without being lonely?

SALLY: What I think doesn't amount to a plug nickel. If I think I'm a goddess and all men are my servants would you bow down to me? If I snap my fingers, would you kiss my feet?

MICK: Would you like me to?

SALLY: No.

MICK: Do you believe in reincarnation? Do you believe in karma and the power of dreams?

SALLY: What does that have to do with the price of whiskey?

MICK: I do. Maybe it sounds naïve but I believe we each have a purpose in this life. In a past life maybe I was too grounded. My soul craved freedom like a junkie craves heroin. In this live I've been a hitchhiker. Here today, gone tomorrow. Don't look back. A rolling stone. It's a long and lonely road but I've never been lonely. I've always looked ahead. The road is my friend and I'm always going somewhere.

SALLY: A regular Jack Kerouac.

MICK: Or Siddhartha. A pilgrim on his journey to Ixtlan.

SALLY: You're mixing metaphors. Siddhartha is Hesse. Journey to Ixtlan is Castaneda.

MICK: You know Castaneda and Hesse?

SALLY: Who doesn't?

MICK: Most people.

SALLY: Where I come from everyone knows Hesse, Castaneda, Kerouac, Ferlinghetti, Ginsburg, Henry Miller, Anais Nin, on and on. We listened to Dylan, Jimi and Janis.

We loved the beats. We were cool and we knew it. So what?

MICK: It says a lot about you.

SALLY: It says a lot about where I grew up. It says nothing about me.

MICK: It tells me you've been on the road for one thing.

SALLY: Sure. I've been on the road. I've been a pilgrim. And here I am. What's it to you?

MICK: You've been on the road. I've been on the road. You've been a pilgrim. I'm a pilgrim. And here we are.

SALLY: Like I said, what's it to you?

MICK: I figured it out a long time ago. I'm a hitcher. I've spent a lot of my time alone. I've left a lot of good friends, good times and good women behind.

SALLY: That's a copout, Mac. You didn't have to leave anyone. You wanted to leave.

MICK: Not if you believe like I believe. Not if you believe in Siddhartha. We're on this road for a purpose. Follow your heart. Stay true to yourself.

SALLY: Grow up. The sixties are dead.

MICK: Nothing's changed.

SALLY: Everything's changed.

MICK: It's still the same road.

SALLY: It may be the same road to you but it sure as hell isn't the same road to me! Not that I'd like to go back. The past is dead and buried...dead and buried. Let's just leave it at that.

[Light shift.]

EVE: I fell in love with a boy. Mrs. Robinson from that old movie The Graduate. Same story except that I fell in love with him. I know how foolish it is. I knew it was trouble. But I felt so close to him. He made me feel alive. I didn't want it to end. I couldn't let go. I'd never known such pleasure. He was so tender. My husband is a typical businessman with two chins, a paunch where his stomach used to be and no passion, no kindness, none. He didn't even bother to talk to me. I had nothing to say that he found interesting. You should have seen his face when I asked for a divorce. He was on the phone to his lawyer before I could complete the sentence. His lawyer saw to it I didn't get my share. Later, when I took up with the boy, my husband made it public. That was the end of it. I didn't care about the money but I did miss that boy.

[Light shift. Silence.]

SALLY: I don't mean to offend you. You're okay.
MICK: Thanks.
SALLY: So that's what you've done? Stayed true to yourself?
MICK: The best I can.
SALLY: And that's why you're alone.
MICK: I guess so. Still, I've always hoped I'd meet someone along the way who was on the same journey.
SALLY: Narcissus to your Goldman?
MICK: Goldman to my Narcissus.
SALLY: Which are you: student or teacher?
MICK: Is this a test?
SALLY: It could be.
MICK: I'm both. The truth is I'm not sure anymore.
SALLY: So what's the point? You meet someone, have a little fun and split up at the next stop. Like it never happened.
MICK: Is that what happened to you?
SALLY: It happens to a lot of people. So what?
MICK: It doesn't have to happen. Not if both of them are on the same road, headed the same direction, looking for the same things. It's a long road. Tourists can't make it. There's no return.
SALLY: Are you on the road now?

MICK: I'm here.

SALLY: Smartass. I mean before you walked in here.

MICK: No, not really. There's more than one way to journey: Sit still and watch the world go by.

SALLY: While all the things you need come to you. Henry Miller, Big Sur and the Oranges of Hieronymus Bosch.

MICK: That's right. I guess you could say I'm hitching through my life, through friendships and relationships, through the stages of life. I gather what knowledge I can and grow as much as I can. Then I move on. There's always something more to learn, something new to experience.

SALLY: [lifts her glass] Mister... What's your name anyhow?

MICK: [lifts his glass] Mick.

SALLY: I haven't met anyone like you in a long, long time. I'm Sally.

[They drink. Light shift.]

BILL: Sex. I admit it. It's all I've ever been interested in and it's all I ever got. Jesus, you should have seen the redhead I had up in my loft a few weeks ago. Well, maybe a couple of months. Who cares? What was it? Laura or Jean? No, Jean was a blonde. No, that was Rhonda. Whatever. The redhead was hot. She had incredible eyes, luscious lips, square shoulders and great tits, firm and round with nipples that stand up and say hello. Nice hips, very nice, but her legs... I'm a legs man myself. She had legs that I'd follow straight into hell! I could've lived with that one for a long time. Christ, maybe I would have fallen in love! Who knows? It turned out she was only interested in the sex. Takes one to know one, right? We had some fun. That's all. I've always had fun. Maybe it was Shirley. No, Shirley was a brunette. Who cares? It was good sex.

[Light shift.]

DIANA: I love the lord. The lord is my savior, my comfort, my everything. *The Lord is my Shepard, I shall not want.* Only sometimes I do want. Temptation is the devil's companion. Is it the devil that makes me want? Is it the devil that makes me lonely on a moonlit night? I lie alone in my bed and I feel desire deep in my bones. I want someone to take away the cold and make me feel like a woman. I desire. Is that so wrong? I think of all the men I've known in my life and the men I might have known. John was a good man. He never found the lord. He tried. He really tried. He drank too much. He left me. [pause] *The Lord is my Shepard, I shall not want.* But I do want. God forgive me, I do.

[Light shift.]

WILSON: Money. Aint nothing in this world worth having that don't begin with money. I'm a rich man, a very rich man. If you've got something I want, I'll buy it. Everything's got a price. It's never failed. The thing is: things change. Beauty can turn into something ugly. The things you desire, the things you swear you'd give your life and everything in it – your wife, your family, your house, your soul – can turn to shit the moment you lay your money down. It's the damndest thing. After a while I figure I might as well keep my money. A while later: I might as well spend it all. What good is it anyway?

[Light shift. Spot up on SONNY at his keyboard.]

SONNY: [singing]
World is full of broken hearted
Don't know why it's so

Love is gone before it started
Don't know where it goes

Somebody buy me a rainbow
Somebody give me the time
Somebody sing me a heartache
Somebody ease my worried mind

World is full of broken hearted
Don't know why it's so
Love is gone before it started
Don't know where it goes

[Light shift.]

SALLY: What do you do when you're not hitchhiking?
MICK: I write things down.
SALLY: Why would you do that?
MICK: I don't really know. I used to think it was necessary so I wouldn't forget. But I never forget. Now I think it's because there are so few of us left: the hitchers. People settle down, grow roots, become trees or flowers blowing in the wind. They're cut off from new experiences. They cling to each other and that's the end of it.
SALLY: They grow. All it takes is love and they grow in their love for each other.
MICK: Sure and that becomes the only experience they'll ever know.
SALLY: Maybe you're right but that still doesn't answer my question. Why write it down?
MICK: People can still learn vicariously. If they're curious they can learn from those of us who are still open to the world. It might inspire a few of them to go out on their own. I write it down for them.
SALLY: You might have something to learn from them.

JACK RANDOM

MICK: I have no doubt. Everyone has something to learn and something to teach, including you and me.

SALLY: Maybe so. Maybe not.

MICK: Okay. Even so, I write it down for them.

[Light shift.]

MARIAN: I fell in love with a dream. When I was just a girl I spent most of my time reading. The other children made fun of me and called me names. I didn't mind. The truth is I wanted to live in those books: fairy tales, fantasies, Prince Charming. What little girl doesn't want to be rescued by her own prince? But I really believed in him. I waited for him. I never doubted he would come. Never. There were several men in my life. I suppose they were good men. But none of them were Prince Charming. [reflects] I've stopped waiting now. My prince isn't coming. He never was. It was all just a dream – a wonderful, terrible dream.

[Light shift.]

BILLY: I was a high school football star: quarterback, captain of the team, class president, you name it. I went to the prom with the homecoming queen. I was voted best-looking, best personality, most popular and most likely to succeed. Those were the glory days! I thought life would be a breeze. Instead, my life has been shit. Reality sucks. Who cares about the touchdown you made to win the conference championship? Springsteen got it right, man. Nobody cares.

I got married to the homecoming queen. It lasted a few years, which was a few years more than it should have. We had a couple of kids. I see them maybe once a month. Hell, I can hardly stand that. I don't know who was more disappointed, her or me. I can't hold a job. I'm too good to be a car salesman, too good to start at the bottom, too good for minimum wage bullshit. Don't they know who I am?

Yeah, they know. That's the problem. They know exactly who I am and that's a loser. High school was great but now it's over. It was all bullshit anyway.

[Light shift.]

MARY: I'm a good person. I can't stand hurting someone, anyone. Relationships are painful. It doesn't seem to matter what you say or do. There will be problems. Someone gets hurt. [pause] I'll be whoever you want me to be, just tell me. I'll do whatever you want me to do. You want to talk about something? I'll talk. You don't want to talk about it? My lips are sealed. Just don't hurt me. [pause] Roy was sweet in his own way. He just wanted to be happy. He wanted me to be happy. He just wanted me to be myself. [pause] Who is that? How am I supposed to know? I've never met myself. No one ever told me who I am. He couldn't say and I didn't have a clue. [pause] Now he's being himself with someone else. We're still friends. I hate that but I don't want to hurt his feelings. He says they have their differences but they manage. They love each other. How wonderful for them. [reflects] But who loves me? I'm a good person. Everyone says. I just don't know who that is.

[Light shift.]

CHUCK: I'm a rotten person. To the core. A rotten, selfish son of a bitch. That's me! You wouldn't catch me feeling sorry because some woman got dumped on. She probably asked for it. Women are stupid. Hey, I didn't make the rules. Every woman knows what a guy's after. He wants a piece of that sweet thing down under. If she gives it to him, she'd better get something in return. If she don't, she's just stupid. It aint the guy's fault. Me? I never stay with a woman for more than six months. It's a rule. By that time

I've hustled her for enough: money, clothes, get the car running, take care of business. *Hey babe, got a job interview. The only thing is I can't go in looking like a bum. Hey babe, couldn't go to work today, car broke down.* Works every time. The thing is, I'm not so rotten that I want to take a woman down with me. Six months. That's it. Cut it off clean. Everyone's got a soft spot and that's mine. I'm working on it.

[Light shift. Silence.]

SALLY: You've gone silent.
MICK: You noticed.
SALLY: I thought maybe someone turned off the radio.
MICK: It's like a morgue in here.
SALLY: So what's the story?
MICK: I'm waiting.
SALLY: Waiting for what?
MICK: For you to tell me yours.
SALLY: I'll show you mine if you show me yours?
MICK: You first.
SALLY: What makes you think I'll tell you anything?
MICK: You've got nothing else to do.
SALLY: I've got plenty to do.
MICK: Like what?
SALLY: I like to play games.
MICK: Shuffle the cards.
SALLY: I prefer solitaire.
MICK: I doubt that.
SALLY: You know nothing about me. You just happen to walk into a bar and I'm supposed to pour my heart out? What kind of fairy tale do you live in?
MICK: I don't want your blood. I just want a story.
SALLY: Something to write down in your little book?
MICK: You don't want me to write it down, I won't.
SALLY: That's right. You never forget.
MICK: You don't want the story written, you have my

word. But that's not what's bugging you, is it?

SALLY: Not really. I'm just not in the habit of telling my story to anyone – no less a stranger.

MICK: We've covered this ground. I'm not just a stranger. I'm one of a kind.

SALLY: You are that. I've known a lot of characters in my life but I've never known one who could give me the time of day. There's no virtue in eccentricity.

MICK: No. It just makes for a more interesting evening.

SALLY: I'm not up to it, Mac. Maybe tomorrow.

MICK: I'd come back but I don't think that's an option.

SALLY: Right. [reflects] I'll tell you a story to pass the time. [breathes] I grew up in a normal middle American home. It was something straight out of Norman Rockwell: a town called Paoli, Indiana. White picket fences, flower beds, green fields, wildflowers, a father playing catch with his son, a mother hanging the wash on the clothesline, a little girl playing with her Barbie dolls on the front porch, a little boy flying his kite. It was all Rockwell, the house, the parents, the town, everything.

MICK: I could have been your brother.

SALLY: But you weren't. Then came Vietnam. Bob Dylan and the Summer of Love. I had just graduated from high school. I was taking classes at community college – literature and home economics.

MICK: [laughs] I was in accounting.

SALLY: Sounds exciting. [reflects] I got involved in the protest against the war. My brother joined the navy, my parents started praying for me and I got out. I ended up in Chicago.

MICK: Democratic convention, 1968.

SALLY: Right.

MICK: I went to San Francisco. The Haight. I hitched a ride to Woodstock.

SALLY: Funny. I didn't see you there.

JACK RANDOM

MICK: I think I saw you. My guess is we both looked a little different then.

SALLY: Patched blue jeans? Tie-dye shirt?

MICK: That was me.

SALLY: Were you the one with the Beatle boots or the moccasins?

MICK: Beatle boots.

SALLY: Maybe I did see you. We made love in the pond by the ancient oak.

MICK: It's a possibility.

SALLY: Maybe you're the father of my child.

MICK: You have a child?

SALLY: No. Don't worry, you're safe. [pause] Where was I?

MICK: Woodstock.

SALLY: Right. I met a man. If not you then someone like you. After a while we got tired of life in the city. He heard of a commune in the countryside of Tennessee.

MICK: Turn on, tune it, drop out.

SALLY: It was called The Farm. Maybe you've heard of it.

MICK: I almost went there myself.

SALLY: Lucky you didn't. The Farm was pretty much slave labor. I'm sure there were some good ideas somewhere but by the time we got there it was all work and no play under a totalitarian leader. A society built on the work ethic that sacrificed freedom. Everyone was waiting for it to change but it never did. I stuck it out as long as I could and then I packed my bag and headed for San Francisco.

MICK: Flowers in your hair.

SALLY: It was a little late for the flower children but I loved the city. There were no men in my life then. I joined a women's group and worked as a waitress. Those were the best days of my life. [reflects] Why the hell didn't I stay there?

RANDOM PLAYS

[Light shift.]

HENRY: When I was in college, we did an experiment with rats. We were studying reinforcement theory: grandma's law, variable and fixed reward schedules, all that. We used these food pellets and trained the rats to press a bar. It was very effective but not absolutely reliable. The rats had to be hungry and when they'd had enough that was it. Then someone came up with the ultimate reward. It never failed and never satiated. We implanted electrical probes to stimulate the pleasure center of the brain. Whenever we flipped a switch the rat would experience pure ecstasy. So we rigged up a flashing light over the bar and whenever the light flashed and the rat pressed the bar: ecstasy. Pretty soon, no matter where the rat was, no matter what it was doing, when the red light flashed, the rat dashed to the bar. Ecstasy. We had some very contented rats. Choice of food or the flashing light, no contest.

We played with it for a while. Sometimes the light would flash and nothing would happen. It didn't matter. Every time without fail, flash the light, dash to the bar. So we added a new element. Instead of ecstasy, instead of nothing, sometimes we'd flip another switch that would send an electric charge to the floor of the cage: pain. Still, every time we flashed the light, the rat dashed to the bar. So we increased the charge, making it more frequent and severe. Finally we eliminated the pleasure response entirely. No more ecstasy, just pain.

Can you guess what happened? Flash the light, press the bar, flash the light, press the bar, flash the light, press the bar again and again and again. Those poor little creatures, one after another, were willing to electrocute themselves and die in agony for that remote chance that the sensation of ecstasy would return.

We were fascinated. We were astounded. And we were

very proud of our discovery. Until one day a funny-looking little rat refused to press the bar. No one could explain it. We had treated him exactly the same as every other rat. He'd just had enough and he stopped.

We called him The King. We put other rats in with him and some of them stopped as well. It was as if they didn't realize it was possible until they'd seen it done. It never ever occurred to them that they didn't have to press the bar.

Most of them eventually went back to the old routine: Flash the light, press the bar. But The King never went back. He'd learned his lesson. That was the end of our little experiment. Until The King came along we never realized how cruel our experiment was.

[Lights fade.]

END ACT ONE.

ACT TWO

(As before. Spot up on SONNY the entertainer at his keyboard. He plays and sings.)

SONNY: [singing]
Yes I'm a lonely man
Done everything I can
Can't find nobody who will love me

Seems like I been before
And if I can find the door
I'm going to leave it all behind me

[Light shift. Spot remains on SONNY, who plays lightly under. Spot up on JOE.]

JOE: I wanted a wife and I got a goddess. Can a goddess even be a wife? Only if she's married to a god. [thinks] She's the only woman I ever loved – before or since. After Marilyn I lost interest. There wasn't a woman alive who could compare. I loved her the moment I set eyes on her. I love her now. I love her with all my heart. Yes, I was a jealous man. There wasn't a man on earth who didn't envy me. Every man would have given anything to step into my shoes – including the President. Who could blame him? Not even Jackie could blame him. Her lure was mystical. I've never seen anything like it. She could turn it on and a crowd would gather. Every man within a mile would make a beeline for her. [pause] After one especially hard argument, she said to me: Don't forget to put roses on my grave. Maybe she was on a suicide mission. I don't know. But I never forgot and as long as I'm alive I never will.

[Light shift. Spot on SONNY.]

SONNY: [singing]
Some people say it's okay
But if I go on this way
Within the night I'm going crazy

[Light shift.]

GLORIA: When he died, I was in such pain. There was nothing I could do. Only love him. *Go gently into that goodnight.* Every night I read to him. *Death is but a dream, an awakening of the soul, a liberation of the spirit.* Every night I spoke to him for hours. I told him not to be afraid. He was a good man. He would awaken in a beautiful place, on an ocean shore at daybreak. Soon I would join him there. I told him there would be other people there. Wonderful people and good souls. He would be welcomed. I told him he would be greeted by a kind spirit, a woman with glowing, golden hair and deep green eyes...like mine. I told him I envied him. My only remaining task on this earth was to see him off with gentle loving care. That done I would follow. He was the only man – other than my father – that I ever loved. Now, I am in love with death.

[Light shift. Spot on SONNY.]

SONNY: [singing]
Yes I'm a lonely man
Done everything I can
Can't find nobody to depend on

[Light shift. Spot out on SONNY.]

SALLY: I met a man. Jesus! All the chapters of my life seem to have the same beginning! I met a man. We got

involved in yet another utopian group. I should have known. Of all the people on this miserable planet, I should have learned. They wanted to start a new community in South America. The leader was a real smooth talker. Maybe you've heard of him.
    MICK: Jim Jones.
    SALLY: That's right. Jim fucking Jones.

[Light shift.]

    JAMIE: AIDS. It's a nasty word. It's the only word that strikes terror in the heart of every sexually active individual in the civilized world. No one wants to talk about it. Little wonder. A single man over thirty? What's wrong with him? Could he be? Could he have been? God forbid that you were ever involved in theater. God forbid that you should be a caring and sensitive man. You might as well dress in black and carry a card: Prince of Darkness, Angel of Doom. God forbid. It's a heavy price to pay. It's almost romantic when you think about it. Every relationship requires the possibility that you'd sacrifice your life for love. Who has that much faith? Given the alternative, maybe loneliness is a small price to pay.

[Light shift.]

    GLADYS: I'm shy. My boyfriend... I still call him my boyfriend even though I haven't seen him in six months. He said shyness is like a disease. The same as gambling or alcoholism. What do I think? I think it's fine. There are too many voices. Most of them have nothing to say. Someone has to listen. The problem is: It's hard to meet people. I don't go to bars anymore. I don't like them. I never did. I work in a factory...in the front office...as a secretary. Everyone I know is married or divorced. The married men don't seem to mind but I do. I joined a church…even though I'm not religious. That's where I met my boyfriend. He wasn't religious either.

[Light shift.]

SALLY: Were you there?
MICK: I wasn't but I might have been.
SALLY: How's that?
MICK: Just like you, I want to believe.
SALLY: Believe in what? Jim Jones?
MICK: Jim Jones, Henry David Thoreau, Abbie Hoffman, Timothy Leary, Henry Miller, Carlos Castaneda, Bobby Kennedy – anyone who holds a promise of something better, anyone with a dream or a vision. There's not a whole lot of us left.
SALLY: Count me out. I don't want to believe anything. I've had it with believing. Jim Jones was just a man who believed he was God. Like Charlie Manson he was a real smooth talker. If you had any faith at all he took advantage of it. It was incredible how many people believed in him. These were the beautiful people, the flower children, the loyal flock. Their reward was the electric cool-aid acid trip with no return.
MICK: You did. How did you get out?
SALLY: I saw it coming. He changed the moment we got to Guyana. It was just like The Farm. He took too much pleasure in being the father figure. I saw it in his eyes. His manipulations became more obvious. Free love. Control of the food supply. Special favors for special favors. I wanted out but I knew: no one got out. I'd seen what they did to people who'd lost the faith. They called it counseling. They were isolated and talked to eight hours a day. No one got out.
MICK: So what did you do?
SALLY: I found my own refuge. It was a place by the

creek. I'd go there after my work was done and wait. I practiced clearing my mind of the garbage, the distractions and all the crap that had become my life. I used to imagine being back in Indiana with my Norman Rockwell friends and family. [reflects] I was there when it all came down.

MICK: It was a long time ago.

SALLY: It was yesterday.

[Light shift.]

DAVID: My friends say I'm strange and they're right. Strange things live inside me. I have thoughts, feeling, visions and dreams. For instance, I'm sure I can read people's minds and sometimes they can read mine. I believe the world is a microcosmic particle in a larger universe. I believe I can fly. In my dreams I travel to far away places. I lead whole lives. My dreams are real. Reality is a dream. If you kill someone in your dreams you'll always feel guilty. Always. I knew someone once I thought I could trust. I thought she understood. I was wrong. Now I don't trust anyone. I may look and act like a normal person but if someone gets too close, if someone gets inside, she'll see me, the real me, and she'll run.

[Light shift.]

JOAN: I worship the truth. Some people have Jesus; I have the truth – as if I actually know what it is. It took me a long time to figure out that the truth is something you simply acknowledge. You don't fall down on your knees and give thanks. The truth is and it doesn't care what you think at all. You can put it on a pedestal or let it be. It doesn't care. That said, honesty is a quality I admire. I try to be honest but it's not something I expect in others – especially in those you love. Honesty has ruined many relationships, including mine. It's a curse but I can't stop. It's a habit I can't break. My whole life would crumble if I gave it up. Like a sand castle when the tide rolls in. Some people have Jesus; I have the truth. I'm stuck with it.

[Light shift.]

ALBERT: Time. Time has governed my entire life. I've never had enough of it. Some say you make time. I could never master that. The more time I have the more I need. I was married once. She was a good woman and I was a good provider. Just the same, I was relieved when she divorced me. She demanded time. The kids grew up and moved out. She had no hobbies to fill her days. She wanted my time but I never had enough. I have my work. I have my projects. Pretty soon I'll have all the time in the world…and no one to spend it with.

[Light shift.]

MICK: You feel sorry for yourself.
SALLY: Who asked you? You wanted a story and I gave you one. That's all there is to it.
MICK: I don't think so. You survived. You've probably been through more than anyone here but you survived. You're stronger than you think.
SALLY: Strong? The years roll by like particles of sand through an open hand and I hardly notice. I'm empty. I have nothing left to give.
MICK: Maybe its time someone gave something back.
SALLY: What did you have in mind?
MICK: Maybe a little faith.
SALLY: [laughs] Faith?
MICK: I know. It's a simple word and a simple concept but it's the foundation of human values and we're losing it. We've forgotten how to say: I believe in you. We've

forgotten what it means to have faith. But I remember what it means. You help me remember. I believe in you.

SALLY: You don't even know me.

MICK: I know you well – almost as well as I know myself.

SALLY: How well is that?

MICK: Well enough. [beat] You're the reason I'm here.

SALLY: That's not funny.

MICK: It's not a joke.

SALLY: [beat] I've had more than my share of wanna be saviors and I sure as hell don't need another Jim Jones!

MICK: Is that what you think of me?

SALLY: I don't know you. I thought I knew Jim Jones. My judgment is not in question here; it stinks! If I thought you were Jesus, himself, that'd be all the more reason to run the other way. I'm not up for taking chances. That book is closed.

MICK: Open a new one. I'm not Jim Jones and I'm not Jesus. I'm just a guy who stumbled into a bar. I don't pretend to be anyone but I know I came here to meet you. It's strange but it's true.

SALLY: The whole damn world has gone mad and here you are. Why should you be any different?

[Light shift.]

CARL: Things happen that you just can't explain. Something buried deep in the past, something crawling around in your subconscious, leads you to where you stand today. My first memory is one of abandonment: a small child in a crowded park. No mother, no father and strangers everywhere. I guess they were distracted for a moment but that terror of abandonment never left me. Ghosts from the distant past haunt me to this day. No one can see them. No one talks to them. But they're very real.

[Light shift.]

VICTORIA: My family was very religious. We were catholic. I used to stay with my aunt and uncle who lived nearby. Aunt Gloria was a sweet woman. I loved her. But I couldn't understand why she married Uncle Henry. I guess it was an arranged marriage. [beat] I could never tell anyone what he did to me. What it still does to me every time a man touches me. I feel his hands. How could a religious man do what he did? How could he take communion? How could he look into Aunt Gloria's eyes and say he loved her? God, I hated him. I celebrated when he died. I wanted him to burn in hell. [pause] I just wish I could tell someone.

[Light shift.]

MICK: I met an older gentleman at a café. I was talking to a couple of friends. They were a couple and I wasn't. We talked about relationships. What else? Why does every couple want to know why a single person hasn't found someone? They're like the Jehovah's Witnesses. It's their duty to recruit you.
SALLY: They want you to be happy like they are so that when they divorce they'll have the comfort of knowing they left someone else to carry the torch.
MICK: Or maybe they don't want to suffer alone.
SALLY: Or maybe they really are happy. Most people can't understand how anyone else could be happy alone.
MICK: You're starting to sound like me.
SALLY: I never said I disagreed.
MICK: That's true. After a while my friends left and this older man joined me. He said he couldn't help overhearing our conversation. He said I reminded him of someone. He said he knew someone I should meet. We talked for a while and I got up to leave. He gave me a card

with some scribbled directions. I figured he was nuts. He was nice but a bit touched. I asked him how I would recognize the person I should meet. He told me I'd know. If he was right, I'd know.

SALLY: Older man, ragged suit, three days growth on his face, one of those old golf caps? [MICK nods] He gets around.

MICK: You know him?

SALLY: If I'm right, he sent me here.

[Light shift.]

JACK: There I am walking down the highway with a gas can in my hand. After a while I start counting cars. Two hundred and twenty nine cars in forty-five minutes. Are people really in that much of a hurry? They can't stop to give a guy a ride who obviously ran out of gas? I'm a normal looking guy, nothing threatening about me. Still every age, race and every other distinction of human being takes a glance and passes me by. It would have cost them two minutes and paid back in good karma but no. What do they think? It's some kind of scam? There's no more faith in the world. People just don't trust other people. [pause] Then, when I'm thinking all this, I start to wonder: What if someone does stop? Why should they be the exception? Maybe they'd take my gas, my money and ride off in my car. Pretty soon I don't want anyone to stop. I'm no different than anyone else. I don't trust people.

[Light shift.]

SALLY: I take it you think the old guy sent you here to meet me.

MICK: Seems pretty obvious.

SALLY: It could be anyone.

MICK: But it's not anyone. It's you.
SALLY: You're sure?
MICK: Does it rain in Seattle? There's a lot of things we don't understand but there are some things you just know.
SALLY: It's not that simple, Mac. Like I told you, I'm out of the game. It'll take a hell of a lot more than some guy with a story to catch my interest.
MICK: I know it's not easy. I wasn't at Jonestown but I know something about betrayal. I was betrayed as a child.
SALLY: I'm not sure I want to hear this.
MICK: Stop me if you can. It's a simple story. I never knew my father. My mother raised me until I was almost four. She was a prostitute. I don't know why she chose to have me. Maybe she wanted to change her life. One day she changed her mind. She left me with a neighbor. She packed up and moved out.
SALLY: You want a shoulder to cry on?
MICK: I wouldn't mind. It was a long time ago but I remember her down to the beauty mark on her left cheek. If she walked in that door right now I'd recognize her.
SALLY: Just like you knew me.
MICK: Maybe I deserve that but it's true. My most vivid memory is of her kissing me and telling me she loved me in a soft, soothing voice. Every morning when I woke up and every evening before I went to bed she kissed me and told me she loved me. I believed her.
SALLY: Every child believes in a mother's love.
MICK: I still believe her.

[Light shift.]

BORIS: I was born a superior man. I came out of the womb with an innate understanding of iambic pentameter and quantum mechanics. By age five I understood Einstein's relativity and Jung's collective unconscious. By nine I had written three novels, a treatise on the theory of everything and an expose on Freud's basic misunderstanding of the human soul. I play three instruments and speak seven languages. All this and yet: I am not happy. It's not easy being a superior being. My parents resented me. It was my curse to see through their pretense of parental kindness and love. They indulged and endured. They encouraged me because they had no choice. The weight of social consciousness prevented them from abandoning me yet abandon me they did. It's not easy being a superior man and in the absence of a superior woman the superior man must live alone.

[Light shift.]

GERMAINE: Do you like me? There's a place between my legs that burns with desire. In all of Paris and in the entire world there is no sweeter or warmer place. Would you like to feel it? Would you like to fill it with your desire? May I touch your desire? [moans, purrs] You like me. You like me very much. I will please you. I've known many men and I've made them all very happy. They will never forget the warm, sweet place where I let them in. Like my mother before me I am an angel of desire. I give happiness and in return men give me gratuities. I can assure you what I receive is nothing compared to what I give.

[Light shift. Enter MS WHITE with clipboard.]

MS WHITE: Miss Smith? Miss Gladys Smith?
GLADYS: [rising] Yes?
MS WHITE: Are you ready?
GLADYS: I think so. [straightens her hair] Yes, I am.
MS WHITE: You may go in now.
GLADYS: Thank you.

JACK RANDOM

[Exit GLADYS and MS WHITE. Light shift.]

SALLY: The air is getting thick in here.
MICK: Sure is. If I don't get out of here soon I'll choke to death.
SALLY: Why wait?
MICK: I though you said I couldn't get out if I tried.
SALLY: You never tried.
MICK: You're a hard lady.
SALLY: What do you expect? I'm here for a reason. That's obvious. Pretty soon it'll be my turn to walk through that door and vanish like a puff of smoke never to be seen again. It will be as if I was never here, like I wasn't born at all. Poof! Gone and good riddance.
MICK: Good for who?
SALLY: Good for me. That's all that matters now.
MICK: It matters to me.
SALLY: Who asked you?
MICK: No one. We're just passing time.
SALLY: That's right.
MICK: What the hell difference does it make? As soon as you go through that door nothing matters. You're history. Less than history. You never existed.
SALLY: Romantic, isn't it?
MICK: How do you know?
SALLY: What do you mean?
MICK: What's behind the door? For all we know it might be a torture chamber. It might be a door to hell.
SALLY: It's not.
MICK: How do you know?
SALLY: Instinct. Intuition. There's nothing nefarious here. We're all just lonely. We haven't hurt anyone. Not intentionally. We're victims.
MICK: Maybe there's a hell for victims. Maybe it's a sin to be lonely.
SALLY: Is that what you think?

MICK: What do I know?

SALLY: Loneliness is a sin? Jesus, you're a heartless bastard.

MICK: It's not what I think. I'm just speculating. I know it's wrong to be lonely and not do anything about it. Giving up is a sin.

SALLY: Giving up is a right! No one asks to be lonely. No one wants to be lonely. No one asks for shitty parents or an abusive husband or bad relationships or fucking Jim Jones! It happens. And if someone has enough of it, it's their right to say: no more! Who are you to pass judgment?

MICK: I'm no one. I'm just a guy passing through, remember? I don't judge. I'm just asking: How do you know what's behind that door?

SALLY: I just know.

MICK: How?

SALLY: I can feel it.

MICK: You trust your feelings, your intuition?

SALLY: Yes! I choose to believe based on my feelings, based on my intuition. Not because I want to believe but because I choose to believe. If I'd trusted my intuition I never would have gone to Jonestown. I never would have gone to The Farm. My life wouldn't be so fucked up!

MICK: You wouldn't have been here.

SALLY: That's right. So what?

MICK: [beat] You still have faith.

SALLY: Sure. I never really lost it. And now my faith leads me to that door. It has to be something better.

[Light shift.]

BOBBY: I love my mother. A better woman on this earth was never born. She was kind, gentle, thoughtful, intelligent, a wonderful woman. When I was a kid she got angry with me. I can't remember what I did. I remember I was mad, too. She sent me to my room where I buried my head under my pillow. After a while she came to me. She spoke softly. She whispered in my ear. She said she loved me but I was stubborn. I held out. Then, just when I was about to give in and take comfort in her arms, she turned. Her anger took hold of her. She yelled and stormed out. It was the timing that affected me. A fraction of a second sooner and I would have been mad but it would have passed. A fraction of a second later and I would have been forgiven. I don't blame her. She couldn't have known that that brief moment would last a lifetime. I don't think I've ever fully trusted any woman since then. Don't get too close. Don't care too much. Don't ever give your heart. If you do, she'll turn on you. Do I believe that? No. But my heart is not as smart as I am.

[Light shift.]

CHERYL: I was an only child. You know the saying: Daddy's little girl. He gave me anything I wanted. Once when we went to an amusement park with pony rides, I fell in love with a cute little pony with a blonde mane. Daddy bought it for me. Dolls, playhouses, toys, clothes, anything I wanted, daddy bought it. I was the first one in high school with a car, a Mustang convertible. I wrecked it and he bought me a new one. We really couldn't afford it but we made do. Nothing was too good or too much for his little girl. He spoiled me and I loved him for it. My mother knew it was wrong and they fought. She warned him I wouldn't be prepared for life. She was right of course but my father wouldn't hear it. I hated her then. I thought I did. I knew daddy loved me best. She was jealous. Now I wish he'd have listened to her. No man can compete with daddy's love. They never could.

[Light shift.]

MICK: You have a choice.
SALLY: Do I?
MICK: There are two doors here.
SALLY: I told you it's locked. There's no going back.
MICK: I don't believe that.
SALLY: Don't tell me: Faith will open the door.
MICK: Yes. Not yours or mine alone but together. One man and one woman. The lonely hearts are here for good. They have no need for the world and the world has no need for them. But we can open it. Two hearts beating as one, two souls that believe in each other. Yes, our faith will open the door.
SALLY: You're a fool, a romantic fool. But as long as we have some time I'll play along. How did you arrive at this conclusion? Did the old man tell you that?
MICK: When I was leaving his company, he said something that stuck with me. I couldn't stop thinking about it. It was my first thought when I woke up this morning. He said: "Doors will open to those with the key. Faith is the key. There can be no faith without love. There can be no love without faith."
SALLY: You're beginning to remind me of Jim Jones.
MICK: They're not my words.
SALLY: They weren't his either. He heard voices.
MICK: I'm just telling you what he told me.
SALLY: So you say.
MICK: You don't really believe I'm anything like Jim Jones, do you?
SALLY: No. But like I said, I trusted him. I won't make the same mistake.
MICK: You just said: If you trusted your intuition, you wouldn't have made that mistake. What does your gut tell you now?
SALLY: It tells me you mean well.

MICK: That's a start. What else?
SALLY: I can't say.
MICK: Yes, you can.
SALLY: It frightens me.
MICK: Name it, Sally. What frightens you?
SALLY: Forget it.
MICK: Trust it, Sally.
SALLY: [averts eye contact] I can't tell you.
MICK: What could be so bad?
SALLY: It's just something I can't say. It's something a woman can't tell a man, intuition or not.
MICK: He has to say it himself.
SALLY: Right.
MICK: All right. Okay. I believe in you, Sally, because I love you. I love you because I believe in you. Believe it, Sally. Believe me.

[Light shift.]

MARTHA: Like father, like son. Like mother, like daughter. When will it end? My father abused my mother. That's a polite way of saying it. And I don't mean he yelled at her or called her names; I mean he beat her. He beat the shit out of her. But you know what? Somewhere deep inside, in a place no one wants to look, she must have wanted it. She stayed with him all those years. Every time he ran out on her, cheated on her, beat her down, she'd cry and swear she was through with him. Then she'd take him back. How many times can a man say he's sorry for the same damn offense and still be forgiven? How many times can he swear it won't happen again and still be believed? Either she had the faith of a saint or she was stupid which she wasn't or she wanted it. I used to believe she was a saint. Now I know better. I'm just like her. She was just like her mother. My father was just like his father. It's in the fucking genes! When will it end? Not today, Mac. Not today.

[Light shift.]

GEORGE: Life is too fucking strange to be believed. My mother wore the pants in my family. My father was a putz. That's right, a putz. You know, like George in Virginia Woolf. Only my father didn't have any backbone. He didn't have any quiet strength. He didn't have any strength at all. He was a putz. Who was I supposed to be? Him? The whole sexual model thing was screwed up from the start. Now I'm all screwed up. I like lesbians. I admit it. I know it's weird but how weird is it? I subscribe to Penthouse Magazine – circulation in the millions. It used to be one out of ten or twelve issues had a lesbian layout. Now it's down to one every other issue. So what's weird? We're all fucked up. We were born that way.

[Light shift.]

SALLY: Why did you have to come here, damn it?
MICK: You know why.
SALLY: I don't. Some old man approaches you in a diner? When he approached me I was sure. For the first time in my twisted life I had no doubts. I knew where I was going. It gave me peace of mind. The last thing I wanted or needed was some fool walking in here to change it.
MICK: I'm not here to change your mind. I'm not here to convince you of anything. You have a choice. All I'm asking is that you recognize that simple fact: It's a choice.
SALLY: A choice? The road to nowhere or the door to oblivion? What kind of choice is that?
MICK: That's not fair. We don't know what's behind that door. Maybe it is what you think it is. Maybe it's something else. We only know it's a mystery. It's an escape. Is that what you want? It's there. Or you can take

my hand and we can try again.

SALLY: Faith. That's what it all comes down to with you, doesn't it?

MICK: You got it.

SALLY: What about betrayal and pain? What about lies and hypocrisy? What about promises that never come true? What about politicians and vampires, soothsayers and spiritual leaders who point to a cliff and tell you it's the path to enlightenment?

MICK: What can I say? It's life. You want me to tell you I'm sorry? I'm sorry. There's always a price and you've paid more than your share. I don't know why. But you've survived and you still have a choice: Go on or give up.

SALLY: I don't know, Mick. Once betrayed, always a cynic. I took a vow some time back. Never trust anyone again. Never follow, never join. I walk alone. It's not easy or simple with me, it's a vow.

MICK: I'm not asking you to trust me. I'm asking you to trust yourself. Follow your heart.

SALLY: You're a smooth talker. There was a time I liked that in a man.

MICK: Not any more.

SALLY: I like you, Mick. It's not you. It's me.

[Light shift.]

SARA: I once loved a man. He was young and romantic. He was a wanderer, a seeker of truth and wisdom, a lover of beauty and a fool for love. He gave up his quest for freedom and knowledge to lay his soul at my feet. He once traveled a continent to my door. He offered his heart. He had the faith of a child. He saw me in a vision, a dream, and I saw him. We became lovers. He worshiped me body and soul. He believed in my innocence. It became my burden to test his faith and his love. I never gave up my quest for freedom, my thirst for experience or my desire for knowledge. I took another lover and when I saw his pain I reminded him of his promise – his vow of unconditional love. He accepted the challenge and I asserted my freedom. I took another lover and watched him suffer. I gave him only a part of my heart and when I held him in my arms I felt more than his passion; I felt his pain. It aroused me. It heightened my pleasure. He was my martyr and his spirit began to die. His faith became the enemy of his soul. I could feel his heart breaking. I felt his shame. His heart finally cried out. He called it the incubus. He didn't know it but that saved him. To this day I wonder what might have happened had I embraced him then. I would never find another love like his and he would always carry the scar.

[Light shift.]

RICK: She was a dancer at a cheap bar. I was a writer of bad poetry. In my eyes she was Madonna – not the singer but the goddess. She was sleek and sensual, bold and erotic, a perfect image of the female form. When she danced she took my breath away. I needed a jolt of whiskey to bring me back. I introduced myself and she was amused. She hadn't known any men like me. She never talked to a man who had more than one thing on his mind. She liked me and I liked her. I don't know what it is with me and ladies of the night. Maybe it's the Lenny Bruce thing: A cross between the Virgin Mary and a hundred dollar hooker. Maybe it's the Marilyn thing: Every man wants to save her. I guess I thought I could save her. Of course that's not all I wanted to do. The trouble is I got to know her and fell in love. Did she fall for me? Who knows? She said so but who knows? She always held something back. Maybe it was her upbringing or the men she'd known but she could never let go. She couldn't trust a man. Any man. I thought we could overcome. I thought my love and faith would be enough but it wasn't. She cried one night. I could tell it had been a long time. Tears didn't come easy. I had brought her flowers. The case with the wedding ring was on the table. She knew. She broke it off that night. She told me an old boyfriend had come to town. She lied. [sighs] I still see her once in a while at the same rundown strip joint. She gives a wink and we trade small talk during her break. Then I go home...alone.

[Light shift.]
SALLY: I want to trust you. I want to believe.
MICK: [standing] Come with me.
SALLY: I can't.
MICK: You can. You know you can. You don't have to say anything. Just take my hand. We'll walk to that door, open it and step back into the world.
SALLY: You make it sound easy.
MICK: The hard part is the first step.
SALLY: I'm not ready.
MICK: You are. Take your time.
SALLY: I'm out of time.
MICK: You have the time you need.
SALLY: My number could come up any moment now. That woman could walk through that door and call my name.
MICK: You wouldn't have to go.
SALLY: No one refuses.
MICK: You're not like them. You're one of a kind.
SALLY: Sure but I'm one of them too. In some ways we're a part of each other. All the lonely people are one: the abused daughter, the only child, the dreamer, the hooker with a heart, the lost and abandoned and betrayed. They're all a part of me and I'm a part of them. We give each other comfort. We share our thoughts, our feelings, our memories, our forgotten dreams and hopes. Somehow we divide our pain, our loneliness, and it makes it okay.
MICK: Lonely but not alone. Is it enough, Sally? Is it what you want?

SALLY: If I did would you understand?

MICK: I would. All these people, the lonely, there's something missing in each of them. They're not whole. Together they can become whole again. Maybe that's what this place is about. Maybe that's what happens behind the door. All these lives are melded into one. Yes, I understand it. I understand it for them but not for you. You're different.

SALLY: I have to get my mind straight. My brain is racing in a million directions. So many thoughts and so little time.

MICK: Maybe it's time to stop thinking. Let go. Trust your feelings, your intuition, and follow your heart.

SALLY: I'm afraid.

[Enter MS WHITE with clipboard. Light shift.]

MS WHITE: Miss Carter?
SALLY: Yes?
MS WHITE: We're ready for you.
SALLY: [rises] Thank you. But I'm not ready. [she takes Mick's hand] Let's blow this joint.

[MICK and SALLY kiss. They cross to the outside door. He opens it. Moonlight spills in. They exit. Lights fade to black.]

END ACT TWO.

ABOUT THE AUTHOR

Jack Random has lived at once an ordinary and extraordinary life. His roots firmly planted in the fertile central valley of California, he has marched the streets in protest, haunted jazz town bars, read poetry in cafes and town squares, strutted his hour upon the stage, crisscrossed the country by air, rail, highway and thumb, mourned at Wounded Knee, gazed into the eyes of the crow at Grand Canyon, and paid tribute at the grave of Geronimo. He has labored in the fields of plenty, toiled on the assembly line, pursued higher education and attempted to enlighten children in the public schools. He has been a pilgrim and a seeker of truth. He is married to the love of his life. All the while he has chronicled his thoughts and revelations in words: plays, poetry, novels, stories and essays.

OTHER BOOKS BY JACK RANDOM

Wasichu: The Killing Spirit. A modern telling of the life of Crazy Horse recalls the history of Native America.

Number Nine: The Adventures of Jake Jones and Ruby Daulton. Jake & Ruby on an adventure to New Orleans in the summer of Katrina.

The Ghost Dance Insurrection. Guided by an Indian spirit, Roman Mason takes aim at a nefarious organization.

A Patriot Dirge. Mason takes on the political and economic forces that control our lives (Jazzman Series).

Pawns to Players: The Chess Series. An elite couple play chess to determine the fate of the American government. Part I: *The Stairway Scandal*. Part II: *A Match for the White House*. Part III: *The Putin Gambit*.

Jazzman Chronicles: Volumes I–X. Political essays from 2000 to 2014.

The Grand Canyon Zen Golf Tour. Two friends embark on a journey of discovery in the summer of 1993.

Hard Times: The Wrath of an Angry God. Not with a bang but a whimper the end of days comes.

Apache Jack: Native Visions & Stories. A collection of short works surrounding native culture.

Random Jack: Tales from Jazztown & Beyond. A collection of short stories.

Aphrodite House & Other Plays. A second volume of plays.

ALSO FROM CROW DOG PRESS

***A Mother's Story* – Stories, Art and Reflections** by Artis Brown Miller. A mother of eight reflects on a life of hardship and love.

Crow Dog Press

www.ingramcontent.com/pod-product-compliance
Lightning Source LLC
Chambersburg PA
CBHW060149050426
42446CB00013B/2744